Why The Black Hole Sings The Blues

Ishmael Reed

WHY THE BLACK HOLE SINGS THE BLUES

Poems, 2007-2020

DALKEY ARCHIVE PRESS

McLean, IL / Dublin

CIP Data available upon request.

www.dalkeyarchive.com
McLean, IL / Dublin

Printed on permanent/durable acid-free paper.

For David Murray and Carman Moore who made my words sing

Contents

Introduction
Reading Ishmael Reed
by Joyce Ann Joyce

Reading Ishmael Reed's *Why the Black Hole Sings the Blues* emerges as a course in twenty-first century modern poetry. This collection illustrates that when we speak of or engage in reading well-crafted poetry that questions our sense of well-being and, at the same time, centers us, we then experience the connection between intellect and passion. A cornucopia of jazz musicians, love poetry, poems about health issues, the motion picture industry, publishing, historical events, racial and political injustice, the maligning of Black men, celebrations of Black women, displaced ethnic minorities, developments in astronomy, science, nature, the loss of friends, corporate exploitation, academic professors, tributes to friends, Africa, hip-hop music, the art of jazz, and poetry itself--the theme that connects this diverse range of subjects is the interconnection between responsibility and the staunch belief in a moral truth. Having self-identified as a "Universalist" in his introduction to *Ishmael Reed: New and Selected Poems 1964-2007*, Reed in this current volume continues to explore his global interest in humanity. Holding the reader to the same standard to which he holds himself, Reed frequently tells us what we do not want to hear. His love of jazz music, jazz musicians, and the culture that defines them reveals an improvised passion for poetry, underscoring a major vehicle that carries and echoes the poet's sometimes satirical, but always non-sentimental moral truths and love of mankind.

With any reading of *Why the Black Hole Sings the Blues*, it is safe to propose that Reed's placing the forty-six page celebratory prose poem "The Jazz Martyrs" at the center of the volume is not fortuitous. An invaluable historical and experiential accounting of what the author of *Piers Plowman* would refer to as a "field full of folk" who make up the twentieth and twenty-first century blues and jazz pantheon, this poem envelops the reader with meticulous details of the severe financial problems, police abuses, failing health issues that resulted from exploitation and abuse, homelessness, the musicians' comradeship, and their passion for their craft. The poem provides the reader, the musician, and the student with Reed's "Criteria for Negro Art," to echo W.E. B. Du Bois. By giving dicta for who the musician is, what the musician does, and what the musician feels about their art, Reed provides us with the principles or mirror through which we can view the poems that surround "The Jazz Martyrs." Because Reed is both musician and poet, we can tease out a paradigm through which to explore why this black hole sings.

A black hole is "a celestial object that has a gravitational field so strong that light cannot escape it and that is believed to be created in the collapse of a very massive star" (https//:www.merriam-webster.com/dictionary/black20%hole). I cite *Why the Black Hole Sings the Blues* as a conflation of Reed's acute ability to draw our infirmities into an imaginative web-- frequently embodying Black cultural music and icons as well as national and international events, historical figures, friends, atrocities, daily activities--forbidding our escape without contemplation that leads to transformation. A significant number of poems in the collection reflect Reed's characterization of the jazz musician as "defiant," "courageous," and "furious." At the same time that these poems underlie the jazz musician's angst in response to oppressive conditions, they essentially demonstrate another of Reed's descriptions of the jazz musician—a "life-sustaining" ability. Poems, such as "If I Am a Welfare Queen," "Hip-Hop and the Blues," "Why I Will Never Write a Sonnet," "Prayer of a Nigerian Official," "Cold Paul Ryan," "The Banishment," "Capitalism Throws Me a Banquet," "The Oakland Developer," and "If I Were a White Leading Man," all in varying ways address how greed, thus money, shapes the condition of our daily lives and equally pose challenges to the self-respect of both the victims and perpetrators.

Although all of the poems above are studies in the connection among economics, racism, sociology, and poesy, Reed places two sets of them back to back: "Capitalism Throws Me a Banquet" and "The Oakland Developer" echo each other while "The Banishment" and "The Return" meaningfully never specifically identify the victims nor the perpetrators. "Capitalism Throws Me a Banquet" humorously addresses the unabashed, merciless, competitive exploitation of the masses and lower-middle class by corporate banks that disrespect, alienate, and overcharge customers, shamelessly offering candy rather than fair interest rates. The voice in the poem, the MC for the banquet, is joined by Direct TV and "A chorus of Hedge/Funds." Securing his criticism at the end, the voice ironically informs us that "Capitalism" bestowed upon him the honor of the bill for the banquet. "The Oakland Developer" proposes a task for many of us who lack Reed's erudition. Somewhat of a companion poem to "Capitalism Throws Me a Banquet," this one challenges the reader's knowledge of American media history. The second line of the poem cites nineteenth century ruthless California developers Crocker, Stanford and Hopkins, who'd envy their contemporary gougers who've priced Blacks from homes into shelters and street living and young people into the basements of their parents' homes. They own City Halls and deny "Section 8/And Medicaid to poor people." At this point in the poem, Reed introduces the name

Thomas Nast that is far from common and only informs us with "Thomas Nast, these times/Really need you." Failure to understand Nast's importance in the poem results in failure to capture the irony and criticism. Father of the American cartoon, Thomas Nast (1840-1902), caricatured William "Boss" Tweed, who ran the Democratic Party in New York. Nast's portrayal of Tweed's greed and political corruption led to Tweed's leaving the country in order to avoid jail (https://www.biography.com/media-figure/thomas.nast). The remainder of the poem suggests that the Robber Barons of the nineteenth century offered a show of support to the arts and that these new developers are such hardened elitists and racists that they do not feign concern for humanitarian projects. The glib tone of the poem parallels the same tone in "Capitalism Throws Me a Banquet," underscoring how "some" neighborhoods and their people do not move beyond the status of commodities.

Two other companion pieces "The Banishment" and "The Return" carry messages with two different voices, representative of the "possessed" and the dispossessed respectively. Using the rhythmic technique of anapest, each stanza of "The Banishment" begins "We don't want you here." This four-stanza poem progresses with the voice of those with false authority moving back and forth between the gifts of hard work, piety, fine dress, educational success of those whom they view as inferior and the failures of those who see themselves as superior. While "We don't want you here" begins every stanza, the last stanza is the only one in which this clause also ends the stanza, emphasizing the complete self-delusion of those "possessed" with superiority.

Neither "The Banishment" nor "The Return" identifies any specific ethnic group, though the voice in "The Return" compels the reader to think of Native Americans and African Americans whose remains and artifacts have been found in varying cites from East to West in the case of Native Americans and particularly in Old City, Philadelphia, and New York. The repetition of "We've come back to" is repeated twice except in the third of the four stanzas. Breaking the rhythm and rhyme that gives this stanza a song-line effect, the third stanza announces the staying power, the strength of the dispossessed who proclaim in this stanza that though they were banished, they started from scratch, prospered "And have restored our/Family over the years." The enjambment in this line represents a consistent literary device Reed uses throughout the collection to stimulate attention to an essential issue as the reader pauses. In this case, we note the rejuvenated staying power of the disenfranchised. The poem "Banishment" was recorded by jazz artist, Cassandra Wilson. Other poems in this collection have been recorded by Macy Gray, Gregory Porter and gospel singer, Pervis Evans. These collaborations were arranged by composer David Murray. Reed regards one of the treasures of his writing career is to have been cited in one of Tupac Shakur's most famous songs, "Still I Rise." "You can buy rocks glocks or a herringbone/You can ask my man Ishmael Reed."

Had "The Jazz Martyrs" not possessed this same commitment to survive and thrive, Reed's muses might have been necessarily different. As defiant and individualistic as the jazz mentors and comrades he describes, Reed includes in this collection "Why I Will Never Write a Sonnet." Alluding to Milton's sonnet "On the Lake Massacre in Piedmont" (1655), Reed informs us that this is one exception to his lack of appreciation for the sonnet form. Milton's poem addresses Peter Valdes (Waldo) who renounced the teachings of the Catholic Church. Some of his followers were brutally tortured and murdered in the Piedmont area of France (https://www.k-state.edu/english233/milton-massacre.htm). Explaining that he fails to see why sonneteers grope "Too many birds, and trees/Too many Hallmark "How do I Love Thees," Reed applauds Milton's allowing his "hands [to] touch grime," illuminating needless and brutal suffering. The last stanza defines Reed's serious poetic identification. He compliments

Claude McKay's making a "Sonnet fight" in his well-known poem "If We Must Die" and suggests that students give "The Jamaican his props" because his sonnet "like hard bop had some spunk/Like Silver's left hand on Opus De Funk." Admonishing critics to take these lines as his concession to McKay, Reed ends the poem, "So take this critics as a bee in your bonnet/You are reading a man who will never/Write a Sonnet." If we listen to Horace Ward Martin Tavares Silver's 1953 album "Opus De Funk," (YouTube), we hear hard bop and jazz that both emanate from Black cultural roots and stir emotions, causing us to move our bodies and contemplate our life experiences as the brother does in Baldwin's "Sonny's Blues." Reed shows us again that his creativity, though it has a global awareness, does not emanate from an arbitrary or deconstructionist sensibility. It indeed reflects the rhythm of Black lives.

As we read *Why the Black Hole Sings the Blues*, we understand the influence of Reed's rootedness in Black experiences and how blues and jazz are portals that allow him to transform musical sounds into linguistic notes. A casual reference or haphazard allusion does not exist in this collection. Two more of Reed's tributary characterizations of "The Jazz Martyrs" are that they are freedom fighters and innovative. Because we frequently think of freedom fighters as warriors who overtly denounce social and political injustices, we, perhaps, overlook those manifestations of revolt that emerge as more subtle. While poems like "Red Summer 2015," "Prayer of a Nigerian Official," "Cold Paul Ryan," and the witty "Dialog" all capture the sickness of violence; greed, self-effacement, and betrayal; the hypocrisy and official lack of concern for the well-being of humanity; and governmental extreme invasion of privacy, the poems "Moving Richmond," "Myron," and "Choices," like jazz compositions carry us to places we would not have anticipated. These innovative poems, like improvisational jazz, make us work. Reed forces us to ponder, to study, and to learn as we encounter the unfamiliar and see the familiar in new ways.

For readers unfamiliar with the Bay area, "Moving Richmond," the first poem in the collection, signals *Why the Black Hole Sings the Blues* proves to be a challenging expedition. The reader's first task is to use the context of the poem to confirm Richmond's geographical location (its identity). A city located sixteen miles northeast of San Francisco on the western shore of Contra Costa County, Richmond's population is predominately Hispanic with Asians and Blacks having a larger representation than Whites who live in separate neighborhoods (https://therealstreetz.com/2018/17/richmondcalifornia-ghetto). A metropolitan, urban area, Richmond has the same woes as any other city with citizens who are primarily people of color. For example, a consistent inquiry on the internet involves the issue of violence in Richmond, which is cited as the sixth most violent city in California. Reed, perhaps, provides subtle guidance for the reader's assessment of the sociological and economic conditions Richmond embodies. Whether Richmond is one of the more dangerous cities in California may be controversial, but what seems to be indisputable is that Port Richmond, a neighborhood in Richmond, is a major shipping terminal, which transports vehicles, oil, and petroleum from the San Francisco Bay area.

The poem begins with "By foot, hooves, cycle, rails, wings/ wheels on chairs, by BART/Moving Richmond." The reader learns that Latinos (the "costumed feet of Cinco De Mayo"), Blacks (who have "moved their forks to peach/cobbler at the Blue Moon"), and Asians (who move to "Dim Sum at the Golden Palace") are participants in a race, perhaps a half or entire marathon. The runners move to the beat of Jimmy Reed and with a rhythm "like the ceaseless dipping of cranes" at Port Richmond. They pass the "old Fox Theater" a movie house that went through several reincarnations. Richmond provided the lenses for the Hubble telescope that provides an image of the Helix Nebula that looks like a "Big Eye." A google search for "feet of Cinco De Mayo" yields the Fleet Feet athletic franchise that has stores in Stockton, Monterey, Modesto, Brentwood, and

xvii

Pleasanton, California. While we can deduce that this athletic franchise financially enjoys the ethnic diversity of the runners, we are left to question whether the runners enjoy the wealth that should accompany their proximity to a terminal that houses/transports some of the most expensive goods on the planet. The final four lines of the poem, perhaps, allude to the poet's criticism. Through the Hubble telescope the world can "see a galaxy 13.4 billion/years in the past/moving/like moving Richmond." Because "minorities" are the majorities in Richmond and despite marathons and the theatre production of the Hubble telescope, progress in Richmond moves "ceaselessly" backwards in the "past," like the repetitive cranes. Black visual artist, Mildred Howard, was commissioned to create an installation for the Bay Area Transit Authority. She chose Reed as the poet for the installation. She incorporated the words of the poem, "Moving Richmond on two mounted iron sculptures. The poem greets BART passengers as they enter the station.

Whether the above reading of "Moving Richmond" approximates Reed's intention may be less important than the inquiry necessary to unpack allusions that comprise a tightly-knit poetic web. His interweaving historical events and figures, jazz musicians, poetic terms, foreign countries, restaurants, political figures, scientific and astronomical discoveries--most frequently with no clues and without immediate reader recognition--proves to be one of the defining characteristics of his innovative strength as a poet, a gift he shares with "The Jazz Martyrs."

Two other challenging poems delightfully exemplify Reed's talent at surprise. Reflecting what Reed informs as the jazz musician's commitment to the love, discipline, and the beauty of art, the narrative poems "Myron" and "Choices" craftily challenge our sense of what we think we know. Reed grounds "Myron" in an academic discipline that appears frequently in the collection: the connection between the science of astrophysics and the imagination. The author uses the poetic technique of ekphrasis in a narrative poem to set the dinner scene in a fish restaurant in which the speaker identifies the restaurant and provides the cultural history to the local environment. The reader learns that the narrator waits in the restaurant for Sonya and her spouse Myron, a physics department head in a university. Myron becomes the actual focus (subject) of the poem. Instead of a fascination with baseball cards, a typical boyhood interest, Myron as a very young man read Einstein and performed experiments in the parents' basement. He now studies applied biology with an interest in DNA, from which a mouth swab is predicted to identify a future disease. The last three lines of the poem suggest Reed's respect for Myron's spacious imagination: "every time I talk to Myron/I feel that someone is visiting/me from the future." Yet, the journey that gets the reader to these lines illuminate that it is the poet's expansive imagination and unbound curiosity that he shares with Myron.

After citing/reciting to Sonya a quotation describing a dark energy force that some physicists think causes galaxies to move apart so quickly that "all the energy will be sucked out of the universe," the narrator glibly wonders what would happen to his archives, and Sonya intriguingly responds, "Cosmologists are given to/hype as in hyperbole." It is no exaggeration here to suggest that Reed, certainly, has explored contemporary knowledge of quantum and string theory. In fact, placing the quotation the narrator cites about galaxies being sucked apart in Google yields 127 results, one notable of which is "Myron by Ishmael Reed-A Gathering of the *Tribes Magazine*," published July 30, 2012. We should not doubt that Reed is aware of the upheaval in astronomical research when Nobel Prize winners Adam Riess, Saul Perlmutter, and Brian Schmidt received the Nobel Prize in physics in 2011 for their theory of the accelerating expansion of the universe. Enhancing the erudition, Reed has our narrator inform us that he asked Myron about Michiko Kaku's prediction regarding time travel. Kaku is one of the most well-known of the theoretical physicists whose publications--such as *Einstein's Cosmos: How Albert Einstein's Vision Transformed Our Understanding of Space and Time* and *Hyperspace: A Scientific Odyssey through Parallel Universes, Time Warps, and the 10ᵗʰ Dimension*--appeal to the literary and scientific imagination. "Myron" evidences Reed's comprehension that the discovery of "hypothetical" particles, such as tachyons in the laboratory gain speed as they lose energy, suggesting that these particles travel faster than the speed of light (scienceworld.wolfram.com/physics/Tachyon.html). Myron shares Reed's ability to take that which is unseen, but felt and conjure it into existence through words in the case of the literary artist, and through procedures that test for the validity of the hypothetical. For both the literary and scientific artist, the imagination is the engine that drives the brain cells. "Choices," another poem I choose to demonstrate Reed's jazz sensibility for beauty and art, reflects the same imaginative energy, yet emerges as enigmatic, provoking us to question what we know about the origins of the Earth and its non-human inhabitants. The puzzling issue involves deciding upon the number of voices or animals that address the reader in the poem. An elephant addresses a "you" at the outset of the poem, saying it is unfair that the unidentified "you" is in trouble "because of/decisions that you had no part in making/something that was decided by your ancestors," adding that the elephant, too, is a victim of "a decision that occurred millions/of years ago." The elephant explains that he asked his mother why he has tusks that the "predators/sell on the black market." He points out that walruses, sea animals, have tusks as well and questions why he has webbed feet for swimming and the use of the trunk. He laments the predators' use of helicopters to poach his ivory. In the second stanza, two lines strongly capture the reader's attention. The elephant says, "We decided to take our chances/on land," and equally as startling is the elephant's question at the beginning of the third stanza: "Would we have been better off if/we had listened to our cousins the whales." Just as Reed does not write a poem that only pays homage to his friend "Myron," "Choices" surprises us by simply not being a folk poem about animals. First of all, a Google search attempting to chart an evolutionary relationship between whales and elephants catapults the researcher into an endless trail of taxonomical groupings that make the head spin with words that describe animals that lived approximately fifty-million years ago. In order to demonstrate Reed's discipline and precision with innuendo, it is essential to force the reader to suffer through the kind of research Reed masters and channels through his imagination in forty-seven lines of poetry.

The three categories of aquatic mammals are cetaceans, which include whales, dolphins, and porpoises; pachyderms, which include mammals with thick skin, such as elephants, rhinoceros, hippopotami; and sirenia, which include manatees and dugongs. Sirenia designates the order of mammals with placenta and includes today's sea cows. The elephant is the cousin of the manatee and of the hyrax because they share a common ancestor. This ancestor is the Tethytheria, a group of mammals that include sirenia (sea cows) and proboscideans (trunk animals). Sea cows are manatees that are fully aquatic with feet that have the same webbed-like appearance as the elephant. The hyrax, the elephant's common ancestor, is a small animal with fur that looks like a large rodent with feet. The whale, ancient elephant ancestor (See *Animals*, Brian Handwerk, "Ancient Elephant Ancestor Lived in Water," Apr. 14, 2008), once walked the earth with feet. The elephant in the poem asks "why I had webbed feet/ webbed feet are for swimming." The whale once walked the earth as well. The whale, the elephant's cousin, warned that the Monster—Man—was "forming in the dark of the Ocean/developing lungs and would soon/ shamble onto the land." The poem ends with the elephant's explaining that since Man, the Monster, was leaving the ocean, the whales thought they would return to the water. The elephant's last words echo Reed's ecopoetics, "I wonder how that's working out/for them."

The elephant narrator above proves to be one step ahead of the rest of us, a characteristic Reed attributes to "The Jazz Martyrs." *Why the Black Hole Sings the Blues* startles us consistently as we turn each page, keeping Reed ahead of us as well. He provides us with poems about love ("Love Is a Natural Feeling," "Love Ballad," and "Carla 77"), with his adoration of specific female figures ("Army Nurse," "The Girl Is On Fire," "Ethel at 100"), those that are operationalized through wit and double entendre ("The Thing Between Us" and "Warriors"), and the delightful, self-referential poems about health ("The Diabetic Dreams of Cake," "My Colon and Metamucil Get Married," "Honoring My Closest Friends," "Those pesky things called genes," "The Gingko Tree," and "The Milky Way Is a Hot Head"). One highly selective poem from each of these categories enhances the thematic diversity of this collection.

"Carla at 77," a birthday tribute to Reed's wife, returns to the poet's fascination with physics. The poet compares himself to a neutrino, a particle about whose nature most physicists agree. The neutrino is an electrically neutral subatomic particle that seldom reacts with matter; thus the poet has no interest in distance from his love (https://www.scientificamerican.com/article/what-is-a-neutrino/). Acknowledging the stability of their love, the poet ironically says that he is "Quicker than Mercury," the planet whose orbital period is the shortest, thus indicating that they will not be far from the site of love. Going it alone would make the poet "A queer particle." The last three lines identify Reed and Carla as "Quarks come in pairs/Like Scarlet Macaws." Telling us that he was born in the sun, the poet identifies with the scarlet macaw, a colorful bird that frequently travels in pairs. Carla and the poet's love is like a quark, an electric charge that combines to form the component of atomic nuclei (https://www.britannica.com/science/quark). It was Reed who identified neutrinos as "ghost particles" during an interview with Bruce Dick and Amritjit Singh published in *Conversations with Ishmael Reed* (1995).

Scholars familiar with the controversy regarding the novel *Reckless Eyeballing* and Reed's comments about the publishing industry's support of Black women's literary work in the 1980's and 1990's will find that Reed's intellectual gaze emerges as complex and humanistically passionate. "This Girl Is on Fire," a tribute to Alicia Keys, returns to the poet's inclusion of jazz allusions and astronomy as vehicle for the message. The title of the poem is the actual title of the song Keys performed at the 2013 Grammy's (Alicia Keys Grammy Award 2013, YouTube). The poem begins with the poet's dismissal of the conservative music that dominated the show, clarifying a taste for "Sarah Vaughn, Ben Webster/and Nate King Cole." Characteristic of Reed, the stanza ends with a test for the reader as the voice informs us of a preference for "Cool Down Papa/Don't You Blow Your Top." The poet leaves it to the reader to know that "Cool Down Papa, Don't You Blow Your Top" are the lyrics to Nat King Cole's "Straighten Up and Fly Right," a jazz arrangement that tells a folk story about the interaction between a monkey and a buzzard.

Reed, always the trickster, uses Nat King Cole's Black folk cultural message as a trope for signifying how Alicia Keys represents cultural beauty and an artistic swagger, class, and the creativity of "The Jazz Martyrs." Keys stops the poet's dreaming as he envisions a "figure in bronze with hips/ by Lachaise." At this point, as with all of Reed's allusions, the reader experiences Reed's improvisational skill. Like a jazz musician, he coerces the reader to pause, and compare Key's chiseled body to that of sculptor Gaston Lachaise's "Standing Woman." Always centered in African and African-American cultural traditions, the poet dresses Keys as a Dahomean female warrior, wearing a helmet with two horns, sitting on a black horse with "ankles ringed with/white orchids." As Keys frequently does in her actual performances, she beats a drum on each side of her, "leading us to war." Reed informs us of the nature of this war in the following stanza: "Nina's lips/are painted on the shield/her heart is on fire/there's smoke in her/ eyes." Like Nina Simone, with the beautifully defined African lips, Keys, too, is an activist, having co-founded "Keep a Child Alive," a non-profit organization, partnering with "grassroots organizations to combat the physical, social and economic impact of HIV on children, their families and their communities in "Africa and India." Keys also initiated "We Are Here," a group that addresses global issues whose purpose is to build "a better world where all people are heard, respected, equal and treated with dignity" (https://aliciakeys.com).

Reed encapsulates Key's fire in an allusion to the Chelyabinsk meteorite that struck on February 15, 2013, over the city of Chelyabinsk, Russia (https://earthsky.org/speed/meteor-asteroid-chelyabinsk-russia-feb-15-2013). Reed uses the historical incident to compare Keys to the meteorite and the Plast Firebird coat of arms simultaneously. Plast is a small town in the Chelyabinsk region, rich with minerals, such as gold, spinel, diamonds, rubies, and other rare gems. The coat of arms for this region is known as the "Coat of Arms of Plast," which is detailed as a "fabulous firebird with green sequin feathers of the tail [and] a yellow bar at the bottom" (https://allrus.me/mineralogical-province-russian-brazil). Alicia Keys emerges as both meteorite and Firebird, representing the phenomenal energy, fearlessness, soaring leadership, beauty, and awesomeness of the Dahomean warriors and contemporary Black women. When the poet refers to Keys as TNT's sister, the pun describes her simultaneously as an explosive force and as someone with much visibility in the magazine *The Northeast Today*, which particularly follows her activities related to economic, health, and social issues that impinge upon South Asian lives.

A jazz artist, Reed emerges as a master craftsperson of puns, allusions, meaningful ellipses, linguistic bridges (improvisation),

and witticisms that echo his talents as a satirist, of personifi-
cation, and self-referentiality. A striking number of poems in
this collection address health issues with the voice of the poet
as narrator: "The Diabetic Dreams of Cake," "My Colon and
Metamucil Get Married," "Honoring My Closest Friends,"
"Those pesky things called genes," "The Gingko Tree," and
"The Milky Way Is a Hot Head," all--as the titles evidence-- in
various ways and to varying degrees, amuse delightfully. While
"My Colon and Metamucil Get Married" and "Honoring My
Closest Friends" entertain through personification, all reveren-
tially address the frailty of the human body and function as
experiential caution for those of us who in our youth gave little
thought to how what we ate, what we drank, the sleep we lost,
the lack of exercise, and the genes we inherit that could define
the state of the body as we age.

I cite below "Those pesky things called genes," a very short
poem that succinctly limns the wit so peculiarly characteristic
of Ishmael Reed:

like you know how people
hold festivals, parades and conferences
to celebrate what their ancestors bequeath
to them
what did my ancestors bequeath to me
arrthythmia

Appearing to some degree throughout this collection, Reed's
aphoristic sense of humor is synonymous with his name. All
of the untitled poems have the nature of an African proverb or
riddle that grounds Reed in an African sensibility now present
in Black folk culture as toasts and the dozens.

When pondering what distinguishes this collection, my
thoughts continue to return to Reed's honesty, erudition, and
contemporaneity. His indefatigable interests, travels, experiences
in academia, love for his friends, devotion to craft, a shy humility
too frequently mistaken for arrogance, and his virtuosic love of

jazz coalesce in this volume, demonstrating Reed's enhancing his talent "to take it to the bridge." The reader who experiences this text carefully might appreciate the following comparison of Reed's *Why the Black Hole Sings the Blues* to a Cecil Taylor performance. In the winter of 1980 at the House of Blues in Washington, D.C., Cecil Taylor walked up to the band stand, knelt down at his stool, put his head down, and meditated for a reasonably short time. He took his seat and began to play the piano. He sometimes looked up, primarily keeping his eyes on the keys as he and the band members played non-stop for at least an hour. When the band finally stopped, I was spent. Moving from Richmond; to the senseless killing of an eagle; to empathy with mothers on welfare; the undisciplined willing exploitation of hip-hop performers; an ode to Billy Strayhorn; the media's maltreatment of Black men; copious allusions to national and global historical and current events; and the opus "The Jazz Martyrs," this collection provides no surcease from the rhythmic pain and joy that flows through our bodies when we read literature that probes heart and mind. Inviting the reader to defy pain with him and his jazz comrades and mentors, Reed still champions individuality and boundlessness.

Joyce A. Joyce
Professor
English Department
Temple University

Why The Black Hole Sings The Blues

Moving Richmond

By foot, hooves, cycle, rails, wings
wheels on chairs, by BART
Moving Richmond
They've moved their feet to the
beat of Jimmy Reed
The costumed feet of Cinco De Mayo
They've moved their forks to peach
cobbler at the Blue Moon, to
Dim Sum at the Golden Palace
Moving Richmond
like the ceaseless dipping of the cranes
at Port Richmond
like the skidding boats at
Point Richmond
Moving Richmond
Your eyes moved to the flicks
at the old Fox Theater
The press gives you a black eye
But you gave the world the Big
Eye
The Hubble telescope
polished and refined
in Richmond

through which the world can
see a galaxy 13.4 billion
years in the past
moving
like moving Richmond

Ishmael Reed, 2010

Gustav

A scientist says that
Crows can recognize
Human faces
After
He released those
He'd tested in labs
They'd harass him
Whenever he took
A walk
I guess that's why crows
Don't talk to
Me any more
Strolling along the path
Of the Emeryville Marina
We used
To be good buddies
They'd do three caws
And I would
Answer with three
And then they
Would do four caws and
I'd respond with four

But now they're silent
I must have said the
Wrong thing
I guess they're onto me
I guess they're saying among
Themselves
There goes that fellow
Who thinks he's one of
Us

I never got as close to
A crow as Marlyse
Her mother bought
Gustav for five Swiss francs
He used to follow her
To school,
And would perch on a
Tree outside her
Classroom
He'd stand on her
Shoulder when she
Went horseback riding

Her stepfather
And brothers hated Gustav
When he flew into their
Bedroom window, the
Brothers smothered him with
Linen and laughed as he
Struggled
After that, the brothers
Were objects of his furious
Pecking
He'd tear out their hair

He crow-sacked the kitchen
Broke dishes
Covered himself with
Flour
When Marlyse returned from
Catholic school
She found that the stepfather
Had shot the crow

She never forgave him

IF I AM A WELFARE QUEEN

If I am a Welfare Queen
Where are my jewels and furs
The baby kept me up all night
No money in the house for milk
The people who got me into this
Send their kids to school in silk
They took the four year old
Away from me
They said that I'm unfit
I work seven hours for
Five per hour
They say that I lack
Grit
If I am a Welfare Queen
Where are my jewels
And furs
My oldest tried to help
Out
They buried him last week
He entered the turf of a
Rival gang
They shot him in the streets
The undertaker sent a

Bill
I have to pay it off
Their papers mock me every day
They say I have it soft

If I am a Welfare Queen
Where are my jewels and
Furs
I travel fifty miles a day
They call it work for fare
My sister tends the youngest
Child
To sleep for her is rare
I try my best to
Make a way
But people just don't care
If I am a Welfare Queen
Where are my jewels and
Furs

Untitled #1

Where do bad playing Jazz musicians go when they die?
The Ukraine

Untitled #2

How are some Jazz musicians like the Roosters
in Sardinia?
It's noon and they're still crowing.

Hope Is The Thing With Feathers

"'Hope' is the thing with feathers
That perches in the soul"
It flies against headwinds that
say No Entrance
to those who want a new start
They came to Ellis Island
To Angel Island as well
To flee from tyrants and death
 squads
who made their lives pure hell
"'Hope' is the thing with feathers
That perches in the soul"
It buffets the confidence of
immigrants
no matter their former abode
They packed them in festering slave ships
and oceans infested with sharks
They packed them in the trucks of
coyotes
but hope gave them the spark
to trek on, with blistered feet
until they reached a new home
"'Hope' is the thing with feathers

That perches in the soul"
It flies against headwinds that
say No Entrance
to those who want a new start

Great Hunger sent the Irish
The Conscription sent the Jews
Armenians settled the Central Valley
The Blacks invented the Blues
The Haitians came to Miami
The Mexicans Las Cruces
"'Hope' is the thing with feathers
That perches in the soul"
It flies against headwinds that
say No Entrance
to those who want a new start
to those who want a new start

Hip Hop and The Blues

I am really Sirius about music
While walking among the ducks,
geese and crows at the Emeryville
Marina
Emeryville,
an old race track town now
paved over by Ikea and Banana
Republic, which are
plopped down on the burial
grounds of the Ohlone. However
you can still play Black Jack
at the Oak Club
My pods switch back and forth between
Hip Hop and the Blues
The Blues drinks Elderberry wine
Hip Hop drinks Cabernet Sauvignon
Hip Hop can be informative and
enlightening, a CNN for the streets
But the corporate kind is to music
what Monsanto is to Monarch butterflies
Not music but a threat
The Blues record the diary of

one's soul
Corporate Hip Hop is all
about the Benjamins
In the Blues
the eagle flies on Friday
The Blues wears overalls

Hip Hop wears
Vuitton, Versace and Gucci
The Blues drive Rocket 88s
and beat up Cadillacs
Hip Hoppers drive Bentleys
In the Blues, a lover's departure
brings out the sweet aching
sounds of despair
De Chirico would approve
On corporate Hip Hop
women are bitches, hos
and skanks
The men are pimps with
furry smiles
Jay-Z has brunch at the 4 Seasons
Bluesmen grease at Smokey Joe's Cafe
Bluesmen meet their women on
rustic Blueberry Hill
Hip Hoppers meet up in
Player's clubs
Hip Hoppers take out
their rivals with AK-47s
Bluesmen prefer Smith & Wessons
or razors as
in Bessie's
"cut him if he runs"

or poison
"nothin in the drug store will
do it as quick as I will" a
warning from Maggie Jones
to a Four Flushin' Papa
"you'd better play it straight with
me if I find another queen in your
deck there's going to be a wreck"

Hip Hoppers are former
latch key kids who grew up
on "Lifestyles of the Rich and
Famous"
Blues listened to race radio
and heard B.B. King embrace Lucille
Hip Hoppers dine on oysters and mussels
Biggie likes escargot
For the Blues, corn on the cob or
a pigfoot and a bottle of beer will do
Hip Hop wears Jimmy Choo
Blues often goes barefoot
Hip Hop's fantasy lovers are
Vogue models who inhabit cribs
in the mountains with two mile
driveways
Blues is satisfied with Fannie Mae
Hip Hoppers vacation in
Saint-Tropez
The Blues take the Greyhound
to Memphis
Hip Hop lives in South Beach
with a yacht docked near a
mansion

Blues singers grew up in one
room Delta shacks
their only companions
a harmonica and
a 12 foot cotton sack

The Diabetic Dreams Of Cake

"Wall Street says that cake sales are low"
or to put it bluntly
"Cake is fizz"
So why is a diabetic dreaming of cake
asked to leave a temple
Because he didn't know that rice cakes
were sacrament
(He managed to jam some into his pockets)
He dreamed that Mount Diablo was a Devil's Food
Cake
He began to munch it down until his path was
interrupted by his Pancreas
The Pancreas had stick like arms and legs
It was frowning
It put up its hand and beckoned him to halt
He pushed aside the Pancreas and finished his
meal
Next, he was attending the Asparagus festival
in Freiberg
It was held in a great medieval hall and before
each person there was a plate of asparagus
He started banging on his plate
Asparagus, Nicht, Kuchen Ja

Next he was running across Central
Park, juggling a wedding cake without
losing a single flake
Safely in some Brooklyn room
the news said that he had stolen
the cake from a tony eastside wedding
He didn't take it all in
He was too busy eating the cake
and watching Julia Childs bake
a cake
He was on a plantation doing
what looked like a goose step
He was twirling a cane
He was wearing a monocle
a black top hat
and shiny black boots
The master said "that takes the cake"
Some of the slaves applauded
Others grumbled and called him a dandy
"You can sleep with my wife and daughter tonight"
the master said
He started running because they were as ugly
or shall we say beauty challenged as well
as booty challenged
Under an old southern pine tree
he ate the cake
He was chillin' with his witch
Not the one with a wart on her nose
and wearing a black cone shaped hat
but a centerfold witch
You've seen her
She was riding his broomstick
while feeding him gingerbread
The walls were caked with

gingerbread, the doors, the
floor and the windows were
gingerbread
Finicky about neatness
she kept sweeping his feet from
the table
but something outside of the window
got her attention
Two blond children were coming down the road
And here he thought that the bones in the fireplace
were animal bones
She pushed him through the back door
but he persuaded her to give him a piece
for the road
Next he was sitting in on a congressional
hearing on whether to classify pancakes
as cake. A conservative senator warned of
a slippery slope. "What next?" He said
"Icing on biscuits?"
His mother learned to make chocolate
cake when working for
a German family
Carlane, whose mother was German said
that the Germans used real cocoa
and so he found himself as tiny as a baby fly
inside of his mother's favorite cake bowl
He was climbing
the ladle to reach the icing around the
rim of the bowl
He and Sigmund Freud
He kept falling backward every time
he was about to reach the top
Now they tell him that he has no free will
that bacteria inside his gut have goals

that don't jibe with his
Or as the scientist says
"Microbial manipulations might fill in
some of the puzzling holes
in our understandings about food cravings"
In other words,
for his microbiome he is just a delivery system that
brings them sugar
For them his body is a bakery
Is there no end to subservience?
He would find the conversation that his cells have
about him hair raising
They crave cake even though
cake spikes his sugar

And so as one grows older
while the external adversaries with whom
you had been feuding either die or
break bread with you
The internal adversaries multiply.
They couldn't give a Twinkie about
whether you live or die

My Colon and Metamucil Get Married

After all they'd been going together for a long time
Everybody showed up for the wedding including
Including old timers like Ex–Lax and Castor Oil

Their vows moved everybody
"I am your Panama Canal and
You are like the cranes that lifted
The wastes so that ships could sail
To the sea," my Colon said
And Metamucil said
"Coursing through you is like riding
A water slide in tropical Bermuda
An all-expense paid vacation"

The rejected suitor Benefiber stood to
The side sulking but after some
Refreshments toasted the couple
"May the fruit of your union
Make Lilies grow"

Why I Will Never Write A Sonnet

The draw of the form I fail to see
The fourteen lines, which poets have groped
Too many birds, too many trees
Too many Hallmark "How do I Love Thees"
(An exception might be Milton's poke
At "the bloody Piedmontese")
Employed by men with too much time
Of noble birth and cousins of Kings
Whose toil was thoughts about the
Nature of Things
Who never had their hands touch grime
Whose Sonnets were roses, were soft
Lacked spine

Claude McKay made a Sonnet fight
So students of verse give
The Jamaican his props
His Sonnet like hard bop had some spunk
Like Silver's left hand on "Opus De Funk"
But even with this I can't get on it
So take this critics as a bee in your bonnet
You are reading a man who will never
Write a Sonnet

Sweet Pea

On December 2nd, 1938
At Pittsburgh's Stanley Theater
a one time vaudeville hall
the movie palace version of Versailles
whose interior displayed a
    4,700 pound chandelier
    12 feet wide, 18 feet high mirrors
    a place where Dick Powell
    crooned soft ballads
    and Cab Calloway did his
    Hep Cat dance
    and whose 1927 opening night
was attended by Adolph Zukor
    of Paramount Pictures
    Billy Strayhorn, nicknamed
    "Sweet Pea," was introduced
to Duke Ellington

Thus began a collaboration that
lasted until May 31, 1967

Those who witnessed the birth
of this creative partnership

were Harry Carney, baritone saxophonist
Johnny Hodges, alto saxophonist
and Ivie Anderson, vocalist

   Duke said to Billy, 23 years
old at the time
"Sit down at the piano,
and let me hear what you can do."
He said "Sit down at the piano
and let me hear what you can do"

   Never one to hide his proclivities
He got through high school
thinking of himself as a "Lonesome Flower"
a "Passion Flower"
Don't real men think of themselves as steel
with arms full of power
who put their shoulders to the wheel
As towers of strength who won't read a book
Not one who could cook for the cast of
Otto Preminger's *Anatomy of a Murder*
Duke said "He became the official cook,
because we had a great big kitchen with lots
of pots and pans. He would not allow anyone
else to enter the kitchen, and he used to cook
some great dishes. He even got himself a
Chef's hat."

That was Billy Strayhorn
whose songs were about the haunted
Those who spend their days
in reverie
who see bridges that can't be found
whose feet don't seem to touch the

ground
missing in action from every day
life
journeying through life without a
spouse
"They prefer the café rounds at night
at come what may places
where one relaxes on the axis of the wheel of life
to get the feel of life
from jazz and cocktails"

In the song he pines about a
break up with a lover but
his real lover would never abandon
him: the key of
D flat major

Billy Strayhorn
Your music could be as subtle as
a chilled martini glass of gin
with a light spray of vermouth
the drink they called "Billy's Drink"
at Café Society
You knew all about wines
Your music could be fantastical
ethereal
Shakespearean
But then it could come at you like
the fist of "The Brown Bomber"
like the score you wrote based
simply on the Duke's instruction
to you about how to get to his
house, 409 Edgecombe Avenue
Harlem

The Sugar Hill of Fats Waller
of W.E.B. Du Bois, Walter White,
Roy Wilkins, Rev. Adam Clayton Powell, Sr.
Of Langston Hughes, Ralph Ellison, Zora Neale
Hurston,
Paul Robeson, Cab Calloway, Thurgood Marshall
George S. Schuyler, Sonny Rollins
Joe Louis once ran a bar here
      Fletcher Henderson
The architect of Swing
He was looking over your
shoulder when you
wrote "Take The A Train"
      And there it was in the film
      "Reveille with Beverly," from 1943

      Duke is doing some fancy things
with his right hand
      Ivie Anderson is jitterbugging in
      the aisle but not before doing a dance
      that involved the bending of knees
      might be "The Camel Walk"
the quickest way to get
to Harlem
"where negro poets and negro numbers
      bankers mingled with downtown poets
and seat-on-the-stock exchange racketeers"
The Harlem of
      Malcolm X and Flo Mills
Of mansions and cheap thrills
      A place where people raised hell
Bessie Smith bailed Ma Rainey
out of jail

"Of Garvey's Knight Commanders of the
Distinguished Order
his Black Cross nurses
    marching
of the Cotton Club, and Connie's
Jumping at the Savoy
    Bert Williams had supper
    every night at
a club on 136th Street called
    "The Oriental"
    Countee Cullen wrote of
    Harlem's "blithe ecstatic hips"
    moving under Sterling Brown's
    "motherly moon"
"Take The A Train"
Introduced in the key of
C major with 4 bars including
those famous 5 16ths
then switching to F major
at the bridge
       "Hurry get on now it's coming"
Billy Strayhorn
Aren't we lucky that you didn't
take a cab

Love is a natural feeling

got me dizzy got me reeling
got me jumping from floor to
ceiling
love is a natural feeling
Sometimes it's quick
like a thunderbird
Other times it lingers like
a hummingbird
Love is a natural feeling
got me dizzy got me reeling
got me jumping from floor
to ceiling
Love is a natural feeling
There was one time when I felt
nothing
couldn't feel that natural thing
I was numb and my limbs were dumb
couldn't get my love to sing
but now I'm back and all on fire
got a lot of love to burn
cause love is a natural feeling

got me dizzy got me reeling
got me jumping from floor
to ceiling
Love is a natural feeling

Prayer of a Nigerian Official

Some pray to Allah
Some pray to Jesus
Some pray to Olodumare
I pray to Chevron
Got me seven Mercedes
To drive each day of the week
all I have to do
is lick big oil
lick it between its cheeks
Kneeling while I do this
I pray for extra checks

Some pray to Allah
Some pray to Jesus
Some pray to Olodumare
I pray to Chevron

Fly my wives to Paris
on a shopping spree
My house is as big as
Mobutu's
a golden toilet
when I pee

My clothes are made by
Mubarak's tailor
My yachts are manned
by the queen's top sailor

Some pray to Allah
Some pray to Jesus
Some pray to Olodumare
I pray to Chevron

Send my kids to Switzerland
for their education
I'm looking out for me and mine
Fuck the Nigerian nation
When the people elected me
I promised them reform
Now they're rioting against me
wishing that I was never born

Some pray to Allah
Some pray to Jesus
Some pray to Olodumare
I pray to Chevron

They carry crude signs that mock me
that show me as the Fool
But who is the one among them
who owns five swimming pools
They dine on that cheap peanut soup
I dine on Caviar
The restaurants I visit
are all rated five stars

Some pray to Allah
Some pray to Jesus
Some pray to Olodumare
I pray to Chevron

They still talk about
that party I threw
It was quite the marvelous event
Women came wearing
Christian Louboutins
and showing off their Sables
Teenage whores from
Saudi Arabia
Champagne from platinum faucets
everything top shelf
Servants from Indonesia
100 prize winning chefs

Some pray to Allah
Some pray to Jesus
Some pray to Olodumare
I pray to Chevron

The big bosses at Chevron oil
are my lords and saviors
I toil to serve them loyally
They give money and favors
They're the ones who've
paved my fast ascent
and who knows
one day I might be president

Some pray to Allah
Some pray to Jesus
Some pray to Olodumare
I pray to Chevron

Army Nurse

She was different when she
returned from combat
Her folks all say she was
The luminous smile
that charmed her friends
was left on the battlefield of war
The radiant music that made her dance
was placed inside an attic drawer
Those corn tortillas she loved so much
went uneaten on her plate
Rumors crept about the town
about her mental state
She overwhelmed herself with tasks
She stopped attending mass
She sent her beau to another girl
gave back his ring and cash
Her favorite books were left
unread
Her only talk
about the dead
of sloshing through the floors
of bone and blood and gore
One cactus Texas morning

her mother went
to see how she was feeling
She opened the door
and saw her child
Her brains were on the ceiling

Honoring My Closest Friends

How many friends would still be loyal to you
  no matter how much you abused them
    How many friends would be with you
    through thick and thin
    Whose devotion to you surpassed
    even that of your own kin
    How many friends would work for
    you even during your sleep
    Who would keep your secrets
    under wraps and would not leak
    them no matter who would seek them
    For that's what friends are for
    Rae Richardson talks to her heart
    Lucille Clifton praises her hips
    that can spin a man like a top
    I pay tribute to those friends with
    whom I have been tight
    real tight for over seventy years
    my heart, my kidneys, my liver
    and my brain

Heart, my buddy
if you give me a couple of

more decades I promise
that I will remove the skin
from the chicken and stay
away from links

When I dine at Mexicali Rose
I will order only the half plate
of burritos
I will do five miles per night
on the exercise bike
well, maybe three
Heart I will strive to keep my
cholesterol numbers reasonable
for that's what friends are for
Heart thanks for the 3 billion beats
Can you see yourself giving me
500 million more
You do that and I will do more
broccoli, lettuce, zucchini and
ll kinds of leafy things

If the spleen looks like a baseball
mitt, the liver looks like a whale
Liver how are you doing down there
in the abdominal cavity beneath
the diaphragm? Comfortable?
I know that you've been working
hard and if I could I would
give you some time off
but I need you to process those
nutrients, hormones,
For that's what friends are for

You're doing a heck of a job, Lungs

You got pipes that
are as powerful as those that
allowed E. Power Biggs to
play Hindemith
You could fuel the voyage
of a luxury liner from New
York to England
(Or at least from Oakland to
San Diego)

Brain, you must be smart
because there are parts of you
that I can't even pronounce
like the Mesencephalon
and what on earth is the
Medulla Oblongata
The sheroine in a Harlequin Romance
An entry into the Belmont Stakes

But all kidding aside
Brain, I know that I have
given you a lot of headaches
but if you keep my neurotransmitters
functioning
I will cut down on espresso

Kidneys
Please keep on
removing wastes and extra fluid from my blood
Control my body's chemical balance
Help me control my blood pressure
Keep my bones healthy
Help me make red blood cells

Heart Brain Kidneys Lungs
Next time you guys talk about
me think of how I have tried to
assist you in functioning for me
I'm no longer playing George
Dickel roulette
I stopped smoking in 1987
I'm still reading books and
learning languages
L'Chaim
my dear Organs
you got me through Diabetes 2
you got me through the Big C
But there's one body part
that had to depart

but wherever it went
it shouldn't be sad
Think of all of the fun that we had

Those pesky things called genes

like you know how people
hold festivals, parades and conferences
to celebrate what their ancestors bequeath
to them
what did my ancestors bequeath to me
arrhythmia

Untitled #3

His brother-in-law went to Los Angeles
To become a comedian
Instead he became a joke

If I Were A Hospice Worker

Africa,
If I were a hospice worker
I would enter the room where you
were lying
I would flick the flies from
your eyes
I would sit with you day and night
I would wash your hot face
with cool cloths
I would spoon feed you
while cradling your
skeletal head
I would
empty your spoils
I would fetch you clean
fresh water
You would avoid bed sores
because I would turn you
over
and constantly change
your sheets
I would stuff your pillows
with lavender

I would massage your
weak limbs
I would sing songs for you
about the time when game was
plentiful
and animals talked
when the forest was the
only drugstore that you
needed
I would amuse you
I would delight in the laughter
that came between your
wracking coughs
I would stay with you
until long after that
day when you left your
bed
And shocked those
who'd given you up
for dead
who'd given you up
for dead

House on Belgrave Street

It has a huge back yard
On the deck
you can see the bay
from here
Before the invasion
whales nested there

The grandmother
a Tuskegee aristocrat is
preparing us lunch from leftovers
She can build you a gourmet meal
from scratch
She inherited her nimble fingers
But her mind dwells in the country of
poetry, which is where the 2 year old
Mia learned her arias, one hundred years
before she was born
The garden has received Persephone's hand
Thriving there are lemon trees, Japanese maple,
apple trees, roses, peonies, magnolia, ivy, camellias,
daffodils, amaryllis, lilies, iris, blueberry bushes,
squash, hydrangea, tomatoes, basil, mint, oregano,
rosemary, lettuce, Swiss chard, a few collards

Though they are kitchen help now
the Guatemalan housekeepers'
grandchildren will discover new
particles and argue before the
Supreme Court

Six year old Makayla shows us her
painting of a shark swimming in
a dark ocean
I play Tadd Dameron's
"Lady Bird" on a side room's
piano
The blonde haired children in
the classic sci fi flick wear the
same black coats and cling
to each other
The members of this family have
the same eyes.
Maybe they are from another planet
too
But they came not to damn us
but to teach us.

The Jazz Martyrs

For Sonny Rollins, a survivor

If, as Ted Joans said, "Jazz is a religion," and some religions have martyrs, who are the martyrs for Jazz? Who are the ones who immolated themselves with heroin and alcohol, got cut, got shot, beaten up, jailed, tortured, denied accommodations, exploited by copycats, exploited by record labels, producers, promoters, nightclub owners, died before the age of fifty and were laid out in funerals where Jazz playing was forbidden like Scott Joplin's wish that they play "Maple Leaf Rag" at his funeral. His request was refused. Or they were buried far from home like Ben Webster whose ashes were interned at the Assistens Cemetery in Copenhagen.

> Jazz martyrs were cheated out of royalties, humiliated on tour, committed to mental institutions and forced to play with bad equipment because they were broke like Lester Willis Young, a.k.a. Prez. Holmes "Daddy-O' Daylie" said of Prez:
> "He said he would go into clubs to work, and they wouldn't treat him as a star...the pianos in some places were almost keyless. He was not permitted to bring in his own rhythm section...when Lester talked about his

working conditions, he was actually tearful" (Shadwick pg.349).

Who are the Jazz martyrs?

Would it be King Oliver who took the coronet to a different place by arming it with mutes, derbies, bottles and caps? He spent his final days broke and sweeping floors in a Georgia pool hall. Ortiz Walton, who, according to Max Roach, was one of the greatest Jazz bassists ever, was also the first black American to play with the Boston Symphony, which insulted him by making him audition every year. Walton's brother said, "He practiced until his hands bled" (Remarks made by his brother at a memorial service held on July 30, 2010 in Berkeley, Ca.). Yet, on tour with the symphony orchestra, Walton was refused entrance to the concert hall at the University of Michigan.

They couldn't believe that a black man would be capable of playing their classical music! They clearly never heard Art Tatum turn Frederic Chopin's Waltz in C# minor, Opus 64, every which way but loose. They never heard John Lewis play Bach. What about Bud on Bach? Both masters preferred eighth notes. They never heard of Fats Waller who said "Bach Me Up." Ortiz was a Jazz martyr.

Who were the Jazz martyrs?

Would it be Fats "Fat Girl" Navarro who played at Birdland with Bird on July 1 and died on July 7 at 26? Chick Webb, who died at 30? Would it be Paul Chambers who died at 33? Would it be Oscar Pettiford who died at 40? Or would it be Art Tatum who, at 46, died the weekend when he and Hamp Hawes made an appointment for Hawes to go by Tatum's? Tatum was interested in Hawes's right hand while Hawes was about to learn from Tatum's left hand. Tatum would always say of Hawes, "You're hot."

And why did Red Garland the master of Block Chords die without a piano in the house?

"Fat Girl" Navarro said of Billie Holiday,
"I'm thinking of when Peggy Lee be appearing in some east side club. Her biggest applause comes when she says, 'Now I'm going to do the great Billie Holiday,' and Billie be out on the street and they all be saying she's a junkie. They had Billie so hung up they wouldn't pay her the right away, they just put a little money in her hand every night after work, just enough so she come back tomorrow" (Mingus, 190).

John Hammond – your grandfather was a Vanderbilt, but in the afterlife we are all the same. Have you run into Billie Holiday or Bessie Smith yet? Have you made up with Billie for ending her gig at Café Society? You paid her thirty dollars for making half a dozen sides. Did Bessie Smith forgive you? You were the sole recipient of royalties from sales of her 1970s reissue albums. You made $200,000 from your association with Bessie Smith, yet only contributed $50.00 to a tribute for her.

In 1947, Charlie Parker was sent to Camarillo to recover from a nervous breakdown. The film *Snake Pit* was filmed there in 1948. "Camarillo was a mental institution, notorious for alleged abuse cases and negligent deaths. In its day, it celebrated its supposed success of lobotomies, electroshock treatments, hydrotherapy and isolation therapy, all of which were subsequently declared inhumane. Camarillo finally closed amidst grand jury investigations." What would have happened to the future of Jazz had Charlie Parker been given a lobotomy in 1947? Ross Russell signed him out on the condition that he sign a contract with Dial, Russell's record company. What is worse? Being holed-up in a "Snake Pit" or spending a year in an army brig? Ask Lester Young.

"Captain Luis Perelman, the chief of Neuropsychiatric Service, diagnosed Young as being in a "Constitutional Psychopathic State, manifested by drug addiction (marijuana, barbiturates) chronic alcoholism and nomadism" (Gelly 100). Young was stripped and searched. He was beaten. "Every night those guards would get drunk and come out there and have target practice on his head" (Douglas 263). He was never the same after those beatings.

Birdland's manager Oscar Goldstein refused to pay him one hundred dollars per night for performing in a club that Young made famous. He died in the Hotel Alvin, a hotel whose walls emitted the smell of dead rats, located on 52nd Street and Broadway, across the street from Birdland. Friends like Max Roach paid his bills. Young Jackie McLean ran errands for him. "Princely helplessness" was how novelist James Jones described him as he played his last gig in Paris. On the plane home, he began spitting blood. Lester Young is a martyr of Jazz. He didn't live to 50. On his last tour with Lennie Tristano, Bird was also spitting up blood. Tristano could play the blues because although he wasn't born dark, he lived his life in darkness, and though blind, his left hand was paranormal.

Who were the Jazz Martyrs? Thelonious Monk was sent to Rikers Island for sixty days even though he was innocent of a narcotics charge. He could have been beaten or even murdered! In 2017, after many complaints about beatings, torture, murder, rape, Rikers Island was ordered to be shut down ending the career of this American Devil's Island.

"Michael Winerip and Michael Schwirtz studied the conditions at Rikers Island. Their report focusing on the treatment of mentally ill inmates—about 4,000 of the 11,000 inmates at the city's Rikers Island jail complex— found that attacks by officers on inmates have been commonplace and that the perpetrators are rarely prosecuted. Alarmingly, potential whistle-blowers refrain from speaking up out of fear of retribution from corrections officers." (NY Times, July 7, 2016).

Monk was diagnosed as a "paranoid schizophrenic" and sent to Bellevue. Charlie Mingus was evicted from his apartment and arrested in the street and sent to jail from where he had no place to go. Or Sun Ra, whom I sat with one night in 1969 as he was being evicted from his Lower East Side apartment?

Who are the Jazz martyrs? Would it be "Little" Jimmy Scott who had to sleep in the Southern fields because no white hotel would accommodate him? He told me this as we toured Europe with the Conjure Band. "Jimmy Scott's vocal style was 'stolen' by the white crooner Johnny Ray after Ray saw Scott perform at Harlem's Apollo Theater."

"Chicago label Chess Records, which later became Arc Music, was notorious for exploiting its artists, who included Chuck Berry and Bo Diddley. Arc musicians signed bogus songwriting contracts which gave the publishing company—and sometimes even the label's owners—the credits and the money that went with it."

Would it be Hazel Scott who, when investigated by the House Un-American Activities Committee, challenged it to: "protect those Americans who have honestly, wholesomely and unselfishly tried to perfect this country and make the guarantees in our Constitution live. The actors, musicians, artists, composers, and all of the men and women of the arts are eager and anxious to help, to serve. Our country needs us more today than ever before. We should not be written off by the vicious slanders of little and petty men" (http://www.jazzonthetube.com).

Martyrs go into exile. Hazel Scott went to Paris. Similarly, when the NYPD, a crime syndicate since its inception, took away Kenny Dorham's cabaret card, Dorham chose exile in Queens.

Who are the Jazz martyrs? Would it be Duke Ellington, who sometimes had problems paying his hotel bills while white big bands flourished? Duke Ellington faced humiliations the way many martyrs face humiliations–with stoicism and calm. The thugs owned the Cotton Club, where black performers were called "niggers," where Ellington had to grin while playing "jungle music." Duke's band members could barely get cabs after a show; when they did, they could only find accommodations in shabby hotels of the "Negro Section." Restaurants in the neighborhood refused to serve them. They depended on a white guy to go out and get them sandwiches at a drugstore. Eventually the store owner found out that the sandwiches were for Negroes and refused to make them.

The martyrs of Jazz faced agents, faced mobsters *and* the police. A mobster broke J.J. Johnson's head when he protected Savannah Churchill from the mobster's advances. The mob drew their revolvers on the performers.

A drunken patron fell from a balcony on Savannah Churchill. She suffered injuries from which she never recovered. Savannah Churchill was a Jazz martyr.

Mobsters forced Louis Armstrong to perform at Connie's.

One night, while on the bandstand, Louis was startled by a gangster who told him a visitor was waiting in his dressing room. "After the set he hurried backstage, thinking one of the cats would be there, but instead discovered a bearded white man who called himself Frankie Foster. Louis quickly learned the purpose of the 'visit' when Foster pulled a pistol on him, ordering him to catch a New York-bound train the next morning. Louis then was escorted to a telephone, where he heard a 'familiar voice'— reportedly that of a Dutch Schultz associate—asking when he was going to play Connie's Inn. 'Tomorrow,' replied Popa" (Nollen 38). Mobsters told Jazz musicians when and where to play.

On April 10th, 1956, in Anniston, Alabama, where my grandfather's sister, Rita Hopson, was murdered by the Klan (my grandfather, Mack Hopson, was murdered for knocking on the wrong door), the South showed the crack of its mean cracker ass. Kenneth Adams and the Vinson brothers sought their white supremacist

53

bona fides by rushing to the stage and attacking Nat King Cole. Busted his lip. Injured his back. Advertisers refused to back his TV show, even though it was popular. He quipped, "Madison Avenue is afraid of the dark" (Giddens 405).

So was the American Federation of Musicians.

So was the American Guild of Variety Artists. That's why some musicians had to end their careers because of bad teeth. They had no dental coverage.

The musicians' unions were just as biased as the record companies and venues. The music developed a framework of segregation and racist attitudes throughout the music industry. Some affiliates of the American Federation of Musicians were as racist as the Knights of the Ku Klux Klan. In the early years, the AFM strictly enforced its policy of segregation.

"The common feelings among blacks as regards to union practices were suspicion because they were excluded and segregated and given the worst jobs if they worked at all. They were very seldom allowed to work the first class hotels or clubs, or even on radio stations. During the early days of radio, musicians were the turntable operators and they kept the logs" (Hayes 19).

Billy Eckstine was a Jazz Martyr? He was barred from playing San Francisco by Organized Crime? Billy Eckstine suffered a broken rib, three bruised ribs, and a contusion on his neck after being kidnapped and robbed. When he got close, real close to Linda Darnell, his Hollywood career went bust. It was the IRS that raided Billy Eckstine's home and retrieved his valuables. A famous friend bought them at an auction and returned them to the singer.

Would it be Lee Morgan shot and killed in front of Slugs in the Far East?

He said:

"This is the tragedy of the black artist: just to live halfway comfortably he must keep on working! That's not to say they don't have any money–I'm talking about in perspective to their talent. These people should have shrines dedicated to them, just like they have shrines in Europe to Beethoven and Bach: Louis Armstrong especially; and Duke Ellington as well" (Salamone 229).

Would it be King Curtis stabbed?

Would it be Jaki Byard shot?

Albert Ayler found floating in the East River? They called it a suicide.

Sonny Murray told me that he was killed over a woman.

Jazz artist Frank Sinatra cut his wrists when Ava Gardner left him, but Miles couldn't get rid of this "Barefoot Contessa."

Jelly Roll Morton was stabbed.

"One night one of these riff-raff got to acting rowdy and Ferd called him. The fellow used some bad language. Ferd slapped him. Then he sat down at the piano and began to play and the fellow slipped up behind him and stabbed him. Stabbed him for the first time in the head and, when Ferd turned, he stabbed him just above the heart" (Lomax 244).

They took his bus, his music, his clothes, his diamond ring, but they couldn't remove the pearls from his music.

Charles Dickens said that you can tell the heart of a country by the way it treats its prisoners. The same goes for Jazz musicians.

During the Renaissance, royalty decided who could play.

For symphony orchestras, the elite of a particular town or city, but for Jazz musicians, the police decided who could have a cabaret card and who couldn't. Parole officers, too.

Gene Ammons' parole officer ordered him to stay away from the music scene, which is like telling black beans to stay away from rice, like telling Vida Blue to stay away from baseball, like telling a mother bear to stay away from her cub, a bee to stay away from a honeysuckle rose. America, couldn't you have afforded Gene Ammons, nicknamed "Jug," treatment instead of sending him to prison for seven years where he was attended by doctors who received their degrees from the University of Malpractice? The favorite tune for the NYPD, which controlled jazz was "Ave Maria."

Is the relationship between Jazz musicians and the Jazz hating police, judges and prosecutors like that between a bobcat and a deer?

A judge called Stan Getz "a poor excuse for a man."

They sent Art Pepper to prison.

Bud Powell, your rendering of the Em 7 flat 5, the A7 (flat 9) and the Dm7 (flat 5) in "I'll Keep Loving You," are like diamonds poured into our ears. In this song and other ballads you showed America a sliver of your soul. And how were you repaid? Drugs to alleviate the pain. Brain damage from a nightstick. Electric shock treatments. Malnutrition and death.

They chained Billie to her hospital bed, she's a martyr.

They beat up Miles Davis for standing in front of Birdland. His crime: standing next to a white woman while black.

"A white, male policeman, seeing a black man with a white woman, became angry and after a few words with Miles, hit him in the head with his nightstick and took him, bleeding to jail. Miles sued the city of New York but lost the settlement on a technicality" (http://www.jazzandbluesmasters.com).

A Neo Nazi coward hit David Murray in the lip as he, minding his own business, was walking through the streets of Amsterdam. A hotel in Germany denied him use of the bath. "We don't allow monkeys to use our bath facilities," they said. Were we monkeys when our kids knocked on doors in the projects after Germany was devastated, collecting canned goods for the "starving people of Europe?" Even when David Murray is playing secular music, the Holy Ghost that resides in the bow of his Pentecostal saxophone won't be denied.

It was America's Gestapo, the New York Police Department, that ordered the Cotton Club not to "cater to colored patrons and not to admit them when they come in mixed parties" (Teachout, 1402, Kindle). W.C. Handy was barred from the Cotton Club even though they were playing his music that night (Teachout,7562, Kindle).

The Police even threw Ma Rainey in jail. Her crime? Loving women:

"…went out last night with a crowd of my friends/ they must have been women 'cause I don't like no men/ wear my clothes just like a fan/talk to gals like any old man."

The Oakland Police murdered bassist Raphael Grinage who was caught in a crossfire between his son and the police. According to them, his son Luke fired first. Their words. Their account. They killed his son Luke too. They killed their dog. And what was the reason for the shootings? A dispute about Luke's dog. This is why

Raphael Grinage, who played with Carmen McRae, Bill Evans, Odetta and Earl Hines, was murdered. He was a double amputee who, not satisfied with being a one instrument performer, studied Cello, Koto and Dilruba. He was killed. Both his son and him murdered because of a dog. This is the account that the Oakland Police gave; they said that his son Luke started the whole thing. According to them. It was all about a dog. Their report.

And we still don't know what happened to Wardell Gray. Left dead in the

Nevada desert. Neck broken. They said that it was a drug overdose. But why did his head show the force of blunt trauma?

Drummer Art Blakey was nearly beaten to death by the police of Albany, Georgia, for not addressing a white policeman as "sir." The experience led him to Islam and a name change, Abdullah Ibn Buhaina, which only led to another policeman asking him his real name, aggressively.

"What is your real name, nigger?" And when they didn't face the policeman's nightstick and gun they faced an all white jury–the critics.

Critics who had Charlie Parker stand next to Paul Desmond on the stage as they named Paul Desmond Alto Saxophonist of the year and a witness said that Bird was standing next to him "sulking, majestically." The critics who named Bill Evans the second greatest Jazz pianist of all time. Bill Evans didn't create ethno-nationalist critics. He played with Miles Davis, Eddie Gomez, Harold Land, Jack DeJohnette, Ron Carter, Elvin Jones, Percy Heath, Connie Kay. My musical Eulogy to my friend Ntozake Shange was my playing of Evans' "Turn Out The Stars." It's not Chet Baker's fault that nationalist critics elevated Chet Baker over Clifford Brown and Miles Davis. Well he might have not played as well as the dozen or more black trumpet players whom Miles ranked above him, but he was sometimes treated like a nigger. Drug dealers busted Chet Baker in the chops. He died after falling from a hotel window. The police called it "an accident."

"After lying in my cell for about twenty-fours I started yelling and banging on my cell door with my shoe. A half hour later I was carried to the infirmary by four guards and dumped, naked, into a padded cell. I couldn't believe it. I didn't mind being in the padded cell or being naked, but it was so cold in there. Maybe that was part of their psychology, to keep you so worried about freezing that you wouldn't have a chance to think about how sick you were." (Gavin 189)

What a burden it must be to have to be Number 1 in everything. Isn't it an impossible challenge to always be at the top of the gonads chain like in the movie "Blues In The Night (1941)" where the character played by Jack Carson walks into a nightclub where the Jimmy Lunceford band is performing, picks up a trumpet and blows everybody on the bandstand away, or "Young Man With A Horn" where Juano Hernandez begs, pitifully, for Kirk Douglas to come down to the Village and boost his gate.

The critics who elevated Diana Krall over Abbey Lincoln.

The critics who anointed Paul Whiteman King of Swing. He said he wanted to make black music better.

The critics who said that Benny Goodman introduced Jazz, the same Benny Goodman who was called by Pops, "that no-playing Benny Goodman," the critics who gave Stan Getz credit for Lester Young's style. Lester wasn't offended. He called Getz, "Lady Getz."

The Village Voice critic who announced that "White is the new Black." Like a mischievous kid throwing a firecracker into a funeral parlor. He said that he knew that he was going to get a lot of letters.

He is one of the critics who've made Jazz criticism a new form of consumer fraud.

The critics who called black Jazz musicians difficult, contentious, unpredictable. Frederic Charles Hannen Swaffer, an English critic, compared Louis Armstrong with a gorilla. Mort Castle described Ben Webster as "An ugly gorilla. An acromegalic, brow bone bulging, lantern jawed, lowland gorilla." Swaffer and Castle belong to a group that denies its connection with evolution, which explains why the glaciers are melting.

They lied when they said that if you gave Bird some heroin he could do classics on his feet and didn't have to practice, but even when Hank Jones, who practiced scales every day, died, *The New York Times* cheapened his death by prying into the conditions of his sparse living arrangements. This offended a letter writer:

"It would be one thing if Mr. Jones had invited the reporter into his Manhattan apartment and had let him see for himself how Mr. Jones had lived. But of course, Hank Jones could not do that—he was dead. This was a clear invasion of privacy and of what is recognized in New York and California and elsewhere as a public persona's right of publicity." (Hoyt)

While Jazz artists continue to be dishonored in the United States, Jazz musicians are still treated with respect in Japan (as our band Conjure was at the Blue Note in Tokyo), and in Europe, where the King of Sweden honored Sonny Rollins and where a French town that Miles used to visit regarded these visits as the cultural event of the year and where, in Freiberg, Germany, they have a Cecil Taylor week. In Sweden, Albert Ayler's fans gave him gifts and flowers. In the U.S. they said his records didn't sell enough. Where else but here would Jazz documentation be turned over to Confederate sympathizer Ken Burns, who did a documentary called "Jazz" only to leave out J.J. Johnson. Like leaving out one of the apostles in a painting of The Last Supper. This depressed J.J. There was a rumor that it led to his suicide, all because PBS placed Jazz documentation in the hands of a dilettante, like taking a person at random, who happened to be strolling by the Met, bringing him in and having him narrate a broadcast of "Salome."

What is the secret desire of the Jim Crow fraternity of Jazz critics? A black free Jazz? An imitative Jazz that is based upon performers listening to records at 50% speed.

A conservatory Jazz with no kick and no bite and no kiss my ass no viscera a Jazz that is as dynamic as a field mouse.

A cleaned up toned down Jazz.

A Jazz with nice Brubeckian chords but no single note improvisation. One of Albert Ayler's band members said that on tour,

"Stan Getz and Dave Brubeck were put up in expensive hotels, while we were placed in rat holes."

Though some black musicians are bitter about this arrangement, others generously promote the work of white musicians.

I saw Jimmy Heath's band at the Blue Note. Under Jimmy Heath's direction, shimmying and enjoying himself while the white musicians on tenor, trumpet, baritone sax, and trombone tore the place up. Including one white woman soloist on tenor, whose solo was full of confidence and vigor; her respect and homework came through.

No it's not white musicians who are the problem. It's white chauvinist critics.

Gene Krupa

warned us about such white chauvinism.

Gene Krupa criticized white musicians for denying the black influence on the art of Jazz. Krupa said, "I sometimes ask myself what the so-and-so would have happened to Gene Krupa in my early years in Chicago if I hadn't been given a chance to learn what jazz was all about from some really great Negro musicians. It would be ridiculous for me to deny this debt, just as it is inane to deny the very origin of jazz in Negro life. Jazz is as much Negro as the spiritual and to pretend anything but that is to fly in the face of fact." Unlike Harry James, Gene Krupa was a good sport, he lost every drum battle that he had with Chick Webb. Billie Holiday said that James came uptown thinking that because of what critics said about him that he was all that. Running into Buck Clayton humbled him. Billie said after that you couldn't keep him away.

I am talking about the exclusive club of Jazz critics, who don't realize that it's easier to write about Jazz than to play it.

Jazz is like chess would be if you were only allowed a fraction of a second to make a move.

By the way, why is crime, black and Jazz, American? George Gershwin denied that he was influenced by black musicians, but then sneaked and wrote a book inscription to W.C. Handy, acknowledging Handy's influence on his art. He wrote, "To W.C. Handy, whose early Blues songs

are forefathers of this work [Rhapsody In Blue] with admiration and best wishes Signed George Gershwin, Aug.30, 1926" I saw this note under a glass

at the W.C. Handy museum in Florence, Alabama.

And could Jazz zones themselves be martyrs?

They closed down Storyville.

They closed down the Barbary Coast.

They closed down 52nd Street because white cops and soldiers objected

to race mixing.

They closed down the Savoy

They forbade Be-Bop from being played at the Kleinhans Music Hall in my hometown, Buffalo, New York.

They nearly succeeded in closing down Minton's.

I remember when Parker changes

arrived in Buffalo. "Lord Johnny" used to come into the Michigan Avenue YMCA designed by the black architect, John E. Brent.

"Lord Johnny" had a triangular snout face like a giraffe's and a trickster's mustache. He wore a long tweed coat. His shiny black hair was pasted to his skull. We were used to blues with doleful gloomy Gus dominants and themes like Albert King's "The sky is crying and tears roll down the street." Lord Johnny introduced us to Parker changes which began with an F major that hit Buffalo like a Spring erasing the Winter Blues.

Jazz is an art that has always had to be one step ahead of the law.

Like Jackie McLean, whom I saw running down

Avenue. C as the narcotics squad was in pursuit.

And they asked me what Jazz has done for me and I said Jazz was like a father to me. It kept me indoors where I listened to Sarah Vaughn, Dinah Washington, Ella Fitzgerald, Bird, Miles, Clifford, J.J., Chet Baker, Gerry Mulligan, Stan Getz, Dodo Marmarosa, Sonny Rollins, Milt Jackson, Lucky Thompson, Jackie McLean, Klook, Kenny Clarke, Thelonious Monk, Art Blakey, Art Farmer, Wade Legge, my mentor, Max Roach, Clifford Brown, Ray Brown, Bud Powell, John Lewis, Lester Young, Lennie Tristano, Charlie Mariano, Clark Terry, Duke, Count, Gil, Roy Eldridge, Cal Tjader, Diz, Randy Weston, Charlie Ventura, Illinois Jacquet, the Heath Brothers, Bennie Green. Terry Gibbs, George Shearing. I wanted to play the trombone like Bennie Green and J.J. Johnson, but I failed.

My parents wondered what was wrong with me. (They preferred urban Blues.) Charles "Merry Xmas" Brown, who later became my friend, who, one day, unbeknownst to me was standing next to me in an Oakland bakery and when it was my time to purchase some pastry said "I'll pay for that" got into his Cadillac and drove away. Charles Brown loved racehorses and was an impeccable dresser. He gave our foundation, the Before Columbus Foundation, credit for his comeback after we sponsored him at San Francisco's Great American Music Hall in connection with the American Book Awards. A thousand people showed up.

Jazz taught me how to dress.

Jazz taught me to be a nonconformist.

Jazz taught me to sing "Moody's Mood For Love," which I would sing at teenage parties to impress the girls. That made up for a shyness that bordered on the autistic. It educated me to trends like musicians converting to Islam. They were part of the grapevine telegraph like the Pullman Porters.

When I met Max Roach I thanked him for keeping me out of reform school. I was too busy listening to sides to get into trouble.

So the martyrs of Jazz were cut, shot, institutionalized, disrespected, beaten and hassled by the police, mobbed by the South's little white knights, cheated out of their creations like Nat King Cole who sued Irving Mills, who made a fortune from Cole's "Straighten Up and Fly Right," sold to Mills when he was broke. The hit made so much money that Capitol Records became known as

"The House That Nat Built." And why does Irving Mills' name appear alongside Duke's and Nat King Cole's on some of the great Jazz classics when he had nothing to do with their creation? When Steve Cannon and I attended a show called "Sophisticated Lady" based on Duke's songs, which starred Judith Jamison, Steve Cannon glanced at these song credits and said of Mills,

"This motherfucker owns Duke."

Louis who had to perform even though he had heart trouble.

Jazz musicians were ripped off, remained unpaid, died before forty, and were treated differently from the representatives of European classical music. Vladimir Horowitz never mopped a floor in his life. Leonard Bernstein was addressed as Maestro. So how come Jazz survives over one hundred years after Papa Celestin's Tuxedo Band

Because it insists like

Sonny Rollins' "Freedom Suite"
Max Roach and Abbey Lincoln's "We Insist"
Lena Horne's "Now"
Nina Simone's "Mississippi Goddam"
Jackie McLean's "Let Freedom Ring"
Archie Shepp's "Attica"
Mingus's "Fables of Faubus"
Mingus's "Attica"
Marcus Garvey didn't make it to Africa, but Randy Weston did. He brought back rhythms and scales in his luggage and got them past Customs.

So why does Jazz, after being shut down, abused, misrepresented, banned, censored, despised, maligned, still hang around?

Because it has the defiance of Charles Mingus who, when a performance of Duke Ellington's music was interrupted by a bomb threat and everybody was asked to leave, he refused, telling police: "If I'm going to die, I'm ready. But I'm going out playing 'Sophisticated Lady'" (Pierpont).

Jazz survives because it made Lionel Hampton jump up from his wheelchair, take the stage and play for hours. Hits like "Flying Home."

Jazz survives because I saw Wynton Marsalis do a Houdini in a place where you'd least expect it. In a Brooklyn Senior citizen's home, where one minute he time travelled backwards to sit in with King Oliver before returning to the present and playing for people, who were dancing at their tables and at the entrance to the hall and down three flights of steps casting Aaron Douglas silhouettes. Wynton Marsalis has discovered the musical wormhole.

Jazz survives because Ellis Marsalis, Jr. dismissed the busboys and carried his own garment bag through the lobby of a Las Vegas hotel.

Jazz survives because Allen Toussaint refused to be photographed if he was not wearing a tie.

They are ambassadors from New Orleans, the cradle of Jazz

where Professor Longhair sang the blues.

Jazz has the will of Roland Kirk, who after suffering from a stroke that paralyzed the left side of his body played a horn with one hand and still blew everybody off the stage. And what about Horace Parlan one of his sidemen who deprived of using two paralyzed fingers on his right hand played with two.

Jazz allowed Chick Webb to play through excruciating pain

Jazz has the courage of Louis Armstrong who challenged the president of the United States to go to Little Rock and lead black children into Central High.

It can be cool as Miles playing Sonny's "Solar," it can be reverential as Duke's "Come Sunday."

It has the discipline and beauty of Ahmad Jamal playing "Invitation," but it can also be furious like the Lena Horne who bloodied Harvey St. Vincent, who called her a nigger, and when the police arrived, she was still throwing things. He didn't press charges.

It has the stamina of Sonny Rollins who even in his eighties is known to do encores that are as long as the original concert.

Jazz musicians were freedom fighters before the sit-ins and lie-ins, and the marches and the mass arrests. Even non-confrontational Nat King Cole challenged restrictive covenants.

When the owner of the Plantation Club told Bird and Tadd to come in the back way, they came in the front way. When they were told that they couldn't drink from the club's beautiful crystal glasses, Bird smashed a couple of dozen.

He said that they were "contaminated." They lost the gig.

Even with tuberculosis of the spine Chick Webb showed up.

Why has Jazz survived when it's death has been predicted for one hundred years? Is it because though they may chain the martyrs, they will never chain the music? Is it because though they may chain the martyrs, they will never chain the music? The Jazz martyrs died to create life in a civilization that embraces death, that hankers for the End Times and gets all wet when it contemplates eschatology.

Whose Puritan
prophets predicted a Doomsday

America
Even your energy source
The thing that keeps you going
is extinct animals
Your fossil fuels emissions
are leading to the death of
the planet
Your invading sovereign nations
and threatening others with nuclear
war is evidence of your suicidal impulses
Why are you so horny for the End Times?
Why do you elect Presidents who lack
an Inaugural poet?

Why do you hate the National Endowment for
the Arts?

What is the theme of the Southern
poem, considered its greatest
"Ode to the Confederate Dead"
all about a guy kicking around
in cemeteries all day.
America, you got it going on
with the grim reaper

Your millions are homeless,
and hungry and you say
Let Them Die!
Jazz says let them live

You even hounded Ella Fitzgerald
and stripped searched Ray Brown

Your Jazz martyrs braved unspeakable
disrespect, degradations, wounds,
illnesses, self medication, but through
it all they were the advocates for life
for joy for ecstasy even when in
mourning, Jackie McLean's
"Poor Eric," J.J. Johnson's "Lament."
Jazz is curative. It brings people out of their diagnosis.
Hearing Jazz, mental patients sometimes come
out of their fogs.
Children emerge from their shells.
Bob Brookmeyer said of hearing Count
Basie as a child
"I melted. It was the first time I felt good in my life. I
was not a very successful child.'" (Ratliff 89)

Echoing Martin Luther King, Jr. who said
"Jazz is Life."
Albert Ayler said,
"I am the prophet who was sent to you to bring
Universal Love."

The Banishment

We don't want you here
Your crops grow better than ours
We don't want you here
You're not one of our kind
We'll drive you out
As though you were never here
Your names, family and history
We'll make them all disappear

We don't want you here
You look too good on Sunday
We don't want you here
You work too hard on Monday
We don't want you here
Your children are learning in school
We don't want you here
Why aren't they behind a mule?

We don't want you here
Your women dress so fine
We don't want you here
Your gain means
Our decline

Why aren't your men
Stooped and bent
The way they should be
They walk about town
As though they were free

We don't want you here
Go away and never return
We don't want you here
Your homes, farms and
Churches will burn
We don't want you here

The Return

We've come back to
Claim our own
To you they're a box
Full of bones
To us they're legacy
Who shouldn't be alone?
We've come back to
Claim our own
Our legacy

You took everything from us
And now we'll take the rest
The spirits of our people
Should sleep among their
Kin
We've come back to
Claim our own
To you they're a box
Full of bones
To us they're our legacy
Who shouldn't be
Alone.
We've come back to claim

Our own
Our legacy

When you banished us
From your town of hate
You thought that would be
Our end, our fate
But we started from scratch
In a different state
And we've prospered no
Thanks to you
We survived your ugly
Taunts and jeers
And have restored our
Family over the years

We've come back to
Claim our own
To you they're a handful
Of mere bones
To us they're legacy
Who shouldn't be alone?
We've come back to
Claim our own
Our legacy

HIT AND RUN

How California has changed
Forty years ago when a pedestrian
left the curb, the cars would stop
Try stopping for one now and
you're liable to get your rear
ended
Everybody is in a hurry
The Big Hurry
"Thou shall still unravished bride
of quietness" of today
is the cell phone
They have turned
Market Street into a
NASCAR strip
with no checkered flag
to stop the cars
Children enroute to Santa
Fe school scurry for safety
Iris Laronda Simons,
was killed here
by someone
who was in a hurry
They didn't even stop

to find out what happened
What was the big hurry
Was their libido where their
engine should have been
Were they using testosterone
or estrogen for oil
Were they all cranked up

Now there is another altar
with flowers teddy bears a
"Mardi Gras" balloon
libations of rum vodka
gin and a sign that
reads "slow down"
with lavender colored
chalk
Someone has written
"R.I.P. Laronda"

Laronda will never kiss her relatives
Laronda will never chat
with her girlfriends
Laronda will never sing in the
choir
will never watch Oprah
or sample Denzel
will never hear that
bird that shows up in North
Oakland around October
whistling a three note blues
arpeggio

All because someone was in
a hurry
a big hurry

She was 26 years old

Capitalism Throws Me A Banquet

Bank of America led off the tribute
"Thanks for your suggestion
"You're right.
"We made billions in profits last
year and so instead of one teller
to deal with the long lines that
wind around the block on Fridays
we'll have two.
"And we'll take up your suggestion
about creating a row of beds in each
bank so that people can take a
nap while awaiting their turn in
line."

Wells Fargo was next.
"We're sorry that we overcharged
you $6000 for your mortgage payments
"Our bad;
help yourself to
the peppermint candy in bowls
placed in front of each teller's
cage."

Barclays Bank said
"Forget about those two
jokers, we can offer you
0 % credit until the end
of 2017, ain't we good
ain't we generous.
"Oh. You didn't read the small
print about the $347.00 transfer
fee?"

Direct TV said
"We didn't know that you
hated football otherwise we
wouldn't have automatically
charged you
6 payments
at $40 each payment.
"But don't
worry, you don't have to renew after
the Super Bowl."

A chorus of Hedge
Fund guys stepped up
to the mic and serenaded me
in rhyme:
"Thanks to you and other
taxpayers for not sending
us to jail to rot.
We're too big to fail"
Their soloist said
"With my bonus I bought
a two million dollar yacht."

Finally Capitalism
Gave me the honor
The bill for the banquet

THE OAKLAND DEVELOPER

O, To Be An Oakland Developer
The envy of Crocker, Stanford and Hopkins
You can pile people into
3000 dollar per month
Kleenex boxes and
Call them condos
If the Chabot Space
And Science Center continues
To run a deficit, they'll
Permit you to convert
It into a condo too.
Think of the ad
"Great view."
Politicians who won't give
You the time of day
Show up at
Your office without your
Even summoning them
They're there to serve you
While denying Section 8
And Medicaid to poor people
They lavish you with subsidies
The Latin word

81

"Cornucopia" comes
To mind, but instead of fruit emanating
From City Hall's horn of plenty;
Yachts, Lexuses, shopping malls and
More condos ooze forth
Thomas Nast, these times
Really need you
In your day the Robber
Barons were
Buzzards
But even they would have
Bailed out the Oakland Ballet.
The 2004 Robber Barons
Don't believe in—at least
Making a show of giving some loot back
They are the new welfare Kings who
Will never be called that in the
Newspapers that beg for their
Ads
Their Mayor Jerry Brown
Will never call them
"Lowlifes" which is what he called
The residents of the Alice
Arts hotel
I guess I am regarded as
A lowlife
My neighbors too
We don't mesmerize the
People downtown like the Developers do

Our street looks like an annex
To the parking lot of Kentucky Fried Chicken
Or something worse
We got Cobra cans for grass

The rumble of constant bass sound
Cracks the concrete foundation of our homes
Some call this ugly belligerence, music
This music sets off our car alarms;
If the earthquake arrived, how would we know?

Last night the local hoods returned
To our garden and destroyed some more plants
In Africa, children don't destroy plants
They identify them
What are they always saying?
That we would have been worse
Off in Africa,
Where the lagbara agbgba are
Revered
Am I better off in Africa or in Oakland?
In Nigeria, I was mistaken for
An Ambassador
In Oakland, I am mistaken
For a thief even while
Shopping at the Zentner
Antique Collection
Some Bee-Londe asked
Me to remove my earphones
After stalking me
Like Dick Tracy
The police answer our
pleas for protection
With a suburban joke
'Why not make a 'citizen's arrest?'
Meanwhile, our children

Nurtured on "Scarface" movies
Are using each other for
Target practice
While the developer's children go
Whale watching at Point Reyes.

Eulogy For Carl Tillman

Carl, about 3 hours after they
put you in the ground,
I took a look at the sheet
for your favorite song
"Angel Eyes"
Did you know that the
bars leading up to the bridge
are the sounds of a dirge?
And that the bridge is
brighter, lacks doldrums
and contains your favorite
line "Drink up, all you
people.
Order anything that
you see."

That song represented the different
sides of you
The party side and
the sad side
the hip side
and the side that admired
beautiful women

You used to sing "Angel Eyes" in
your cool style like the
soloists with Kenton's band
like June Christy
You sounded like Chet Baker
I added a note to the white
flowers that I sent.
"We lit up the town."
maybe that's why the
woman who informed me
of your death laughed when
she said that you told her about
our history
It is true
we liked to party
our favorites were
low-down dives like
"The Little Paris" and all of the other
places where if you said the
wrong thing you could
find your guts spilling
out
We partied with anybody we
liked which earned us a tail from
the Buffalo police who wanted
to quarantine us
keep us out of the hair of
white neighborhoods
But in between the parties
we studied Philosophy
Music, read Dostoyevsky
and T.S. Eliot's poetry out
loud, I road to the University
of Buffalo on a bicycle

one day a car full of white
kids pulled up alongside
me and called me a nigger

We weren't wild
We just liked to have a good time
cheap
You were the best dancer the
way you moved your feet
scratching your sides as you
kicked out to the blues
And when the dives closed
we'd hit the after hours joints
seeking something stronger
and the woman who ran the place
asked me about Sappho.
That was the B part of that
song, but

Carl, you were tall
tall like you must have
gotten tired of all the jokes
like "How's the weather up there."
Even JFK looked up to you
as he walked past the two
of us without a single escort
because they'd changed his exit
1959 a campaign rally at
War Memorial Auditorium

I was with you when the kid asked
"Mr. are you a giant?" and the kid
ran off when you said
"Yes and I eat little children"

Guess you had enough but
we never got enough
Our appetites were enormous
Some people died when drinking
our favorite drink
"Purple Passion"
Thunderbird mixed with Vodka

They were curious about your length
but you had a tall mind as well

You were writing novels in high school
and listening to Tchaikovsky

We thought that there was no
expiration date on our youth

Like you probably don't
fit the box they lay you in
like we didn't let Buffalo
box us into the boundaries
that racism confined us
Eagle Street was our South
West Ferry was our North
East Utica was our East
And Jefferson Avenue our West
Beyond those limits, you might
Get a beating

We despised our middle class
peers
we jeered at cotillions and
wore sneakers on Easter
refused to join a fraternity
or sorority

We were some strange Negroes
to those who pledged to sororities
and fraternities
We'd rather act in plays by
Jean Anouilh, Tennessee Williams
We were members of
a genius circle that included
Ray Smith Buffalo's Harry Belafonte
Fred Clifton smarter than Socrates
Lucille who won a National Book Award
Claude Walker whose jazz genius burned him
up. Here was a kid who played hard bop
before it entered the jazz lexicon. He'd
disappear for a while. Why? He was a soloist
with the Eastman Symphony and there
was
Philip Wooby who translated Lucretius
at nineteen and received a Prix De Rome
Beautiful Priscilla of the High I.Q.
Teddy Jackson who when I met him
said
"You mean you haven't read Beckett?"
It's Saturday night
I'm writing this eulogy
sitting at the kitchen table
and playing the radio
Muddy Waters is singing

"Blow Wind Blow Wind
Blow My Baby Back To Me"
I'm thinking about our circle
diminished by death
Thinking about you singing
"Angel Eyes," the musical kissing cousin of
"St. James Infirmary"

Untitled #4

When his in laws ask
him to visit them
he doesn't know whether
it's an invitation or a
subpoena.

The Missionaries

We don't have the regalia
Of thunder voiced Mahalia
We don't have the eloquence
Of John or Paul
We do our mission
Among the ones who
Listen

We make a joyful noise*
Unto the lord

We know the dance steps
Of the prophet Miriam**
We have the ram's horn
That's heard by God
Our rolling drums call
An Army of the faithful

We make a joyful noise
Unto the lord

We play to outcasts
We play in rich men's

Parlors
We play to workers
To lift their toil
Our flutes and oboes
Can heal the souls that've
Been torn
Our charging
Saxophones
Can reach those unborn

We clap our hands
We stomp our feet
We make a joyful noise
Unto the lord

*Psalm 98

** Miriam, a prophet and sister of Moses leads the
Israelites in dance after they've crossed the Red Sea

Mino Woman

The French called you Amazon
You called yourself the Mino
Guardian of King Agadja
Daughter of Ayaba and Loko
You have never been with a man
Mino woman
Whose creator is Nana Buluku
When the elephants see you
They turn and run in the opposite direction
Mino woman
You ride into town on the back
of Sogbo
Here, have some Gin
Mino woman
Devotee of Mami Wata
what is that you are holding by
its hair, a Frenchman's head?
Mino woman
you dance on the snout of
a crocodile
Mino woman
You have never slept with a man
Mino woman

Damballah slithers into
your bed your body is his playground
Here I have brought you this
shiny bracelet.
Mino woman
you raided our village
Mino woman
you sold my father for a musket

Scrub Jays

Free as a bird
You wish
Grounded
And cross old man
Glaring from the
Kitchen window
As I stab my beak into
The choice apples at
The top of your tree
You can ball your fists
All you want
You can grit your
Plastic teeth
But there's nothing that
You can do about it

What good are apples
To old men anyway
You have lost your bite
You have run out of
Ladders to climb

Your ultrasonic solar powered
Animal repellent
The Honda among dissuaders
Might rid your garden of
The capo cats but
The bandit raccoons
 Figured out that one
 Within 48 hours

Getting rid of one pest
Only invites others
You're in your seventies
And haven't learned that

Now that the coast
Is clear, our entire
Family can fly in
I know
We are warble less
We are born thieves
We'll steal an acorn
From a woodpecker

We've beaten you out
Of your harvest
We, who are not the decorous
Fluorescent songbird of your
Dreams

Myron

We lunch at Spenger's
a Berkeley fresh fish grotto built on
Ohlone bones and tall tales
about marlins that fought for
hours
Dining in this place is like
dining on "The Sea Hawk" (1940)
but we aren't moving, but
maybe we are
By the time we finish lunch
the earth will have traveled
6500 miles
and don't expect Errol Flynn, in
pirate costume, to swashbuckle
across the floor, nor do swords
cross at this site, only knives
and forks, going at the mussels
clams and shrimp

It is rumored that
Clark Gable once sampled
the famous clam chowder of
this restaurant where a

a Polynesian wood "idol"
greets the diners

Myron and Sonya have
joined us
I'm having blackened catfish
They pry their meals from
shells
They've stopped off in
Berkeley on the way to
SFO
His destination is Dallas
He heads a department
of physics there

She's going to Santa Fe
to inspect their new home

I overheard two shaggy
professors, old, soft and retired argue
about science in the men's locker
room at the Berkeley Y
One said that science is
only a method and
that science can't
explain gravity
I can
Sonya is gravity
And not even chemo or
infusions can
come between her and her
students as she fights an
invader like the Russians
fought at Leningrad

I imagine Myron as a youngster
While his friends are trading baseball
cards
He's reading Einstein
and making experiments
in his parents' basement
His Mom and Dad would call
these experiments
explosions

He's studying applied biology
because
soon he says they will be able
to swab the inside of your
mouth and with
the DNA collected predict
diseases
to which one is prone ,
and prescribe medication

He says that the universe's speed is
accelerating and I read
"If the universe continues accelerating, astronomers
say, rather than coasting gently into the night, distant
galaxies will eventually be moving apart so quickly
that they cannot communicate with one another and
all the energy will be sucked out of the universe"
and I'm thinking,
If this happens
what will become of my
archives? but Sonya
reassures me
"Cosmologists are given to
hype as in hyperbole"

I ask Myron
about Michiko Kaku's
prediction that
time travel will enable a
person's descendants to visit
that person

Hong Kong scientists
dispute the idea
They say that they
have proved that
a single photon obeys
Einstein's theory
that nothing can travel faster
than the speed of light
I think they're wrong because
every time I talk to Myron
I feel that someone is visiting
me from the future.

Be My Monster, love

I've left the window half open
climb in, my neck is yours
suck me until I'm anemic
until I can't get out of bed
until the doctors give me up for dead
till there's nothing left to feel
Leave a whiff of your
sultry cologne
so I'll know that you're real
so I'll know that you're real

Be my monster, love
we don't have to wait for
no full moon
Let your hair grow long
Let your fingernails become
claws
You're my Wolf Man
I'm your Cat Woman
I don't care about your flaws
make me
scratch and scream
and hiss and purr

Rip off my blanket
cover me with your fur
cover me with your fur

Be My Monster Love
You ain't no poltergeist
you just shy
saying that you love me
by making plates fly
using my mirror to
write weird rhymes
Just show me yours and
I'll show you mine
Just show me yours and
I'll show you mine

Be My Monster Love
Like Hannibal Lecter
Take a hot piece out of me
and roll me on your tongue
savor all of my delicacies
till you're good and done
and when you're all through
Give me some
Give me some

Be My Monster love
The mummy of my dreams
come, lift me from my
bed of flowers
come on now
and carry me to my
King
Be my Monster love
Carry me to my King

Choices

Is it unfair that you are in trouble because of
decisions that you had no part in the making
something that was decided by your ancestors
in my case, a decision that occurred millions
of years ago
I kept asking my mother
why I had these tusks, which predators
sell on the black market
I've noticed that walruses, which
are sea animals, have tusks
She said that tusks are used to
impale your enemies
I asked why I had webbed feet
webbed feet are for swimming

Even she has forgotten
And now our numbers are diminishing
down 60% in a short time
We used to dissuade our enemies with
a good whack from our trunks or
by charging them
Or stepping on them or terrifying them
with our terrible cry

We used our trunks to pick them
up and fling them about
We decided to take our chances
on the land
But now they kill us from helicopters
Our ivory enhances their bottom line
And want to know the latest?
They want to create a mechanical trunk
that will duplicate our sense of smell

Would we have been better off if
we had listened to our cousins the whales
who can not only swim long distances
but can see ahead long distances into
the future
They warned us that the Monster was
forming in the dark of the Ocean
developing lungs and would soon
shamble onto the land

not only threatening it's life but all life
Since the Monster was leaving the ocean
they thought that it would be safe
for them to leave the land and
settle there
I wonder how that's working out
for them

If I Were A White Leading Man

I could be like David Kepesh in "Elegy"
and Consuela Castillo would
romp about
my apartment in the nude
while I played Satie and
quoted Great Books
She's thirty years younger than I
If I were a white leading man
I could be Hank Grotowski
exhausting myself over
Leticia Musgrove
whipping it on that thing
and nobody would make nothing
of it
I was her husband's
executioner, yet there's
still a happy ending
after all
He was a no good nigger
not Steven Spielberg or
Menno Meyjes's
no good incest nigger
not Harvey Weinstein's

bad incest nigger
David Mamet's
no good old pimpin' nigger
and not even George
Pelecanos, David Simon
and Richard Price's no
good crack niggers
not even HBO and CNN's
no good mugging niggers
But in "Monster's Ball"
a no good death row nigger
played by Puffy Sean Combs
Next to him Hank is a Saint
If I were a white leading man
I could be like Leonard Chess
in "Cadillac Records" and
Etta James would have the hots for me
and nobody would accuse her of
having Nordic Fever
Nobody would give it
a second thought
They'd say
what's the big deal?
I had to supervise the unruly
lives of her and Muddy Waters
Niggers in trouble. Always getting
me out of bed to bail them out
of a jam
always low on cash
The White Man's Burden
I could be like Adrien Brody
French kiss Halle Berry
while dipping her to the floor
at the Oscars and not a single

hate blog would be posted
Marisa Ventura
would serve me
in "Maid In Manhattan"
and be grateful if I so much
as gave her the time of day
I'm Christopher Marshall
John Barrymore and I
have the same profile
I could be like Major John Blackthorne
in "Shogun"
I know more about the Samurai
tradition than the Japanese
In the movie poster
I'm shielding
Lady Toda Buntaro - Mariko
and nobody would send me
letters about acting white
yet sleeping yellow
(in the movie ads
I'm always the center
my women and minority
sidekicks at the margins)
I'd be
protecting her
like Phil Spector
rescued Tina Turner
in "What's Love Got To
Do With It"
directed by Brian Gibson
script by Kurt Loder
a no good domestic abusing
nigger
the one whose "Rocket 88"

made him thousands while
those who "borrowed" from
him made hundreds of millions
The Times obituary called him
an "ogre"
If I were a white leading man
I would be Harry Lesser in
"The Tenants"
All of the women in the
film the black ones and
the white ones would be
hittin' on me
Niki J. Crawford and
Irene Bell
I would capture Irene
Bell from the claws of
Willie Spearmint
He wants to be a writer
that's a laugh
He's played by
Snoop Dogg
I'm so fine
I'm so audacious
I'm so full of myself
I'm Jim Luther Davis
in "Harsh Times"
When I return to visit an old
flame, a Latina named Letty
I can bust into her house
despite her sister's objections
make out with her
and when her Chicano boyfriend
shows up
I'll Ninja his wetback ass and take down

his greaser posse even though
I'm just one guy well two maybe
(Mike Alonzo assists me
a brown instead of the usual
black sidekick)
After all, guys like me
inspired "Superman" "Bat Man"
"Spider Man" "The Green Hornet"
"The Shadow Knows"
We invented the "Bossa Nova"
"Tex Mex"
"Jazz" "Rock and Roll"
As Sheriff Sam Deeds in
"Lone Star," I would make
Pilar, another
Chicana beauty
"Forget about the Alamo"
as I am about to lay a hard
one on her
and nobody would accuse me
of betraying my race
In fact, I would get some
man love from my peers
after all
"Black juice makes a man
of you" as Hank's
father Buck Grotowski says
in "Monster's Ball"
Apparently that goes for yellow
juice, brown juice, and
red juice and whatever juice
I could be Rich Shields
in "The Joy Luck Club"
The Asian American

brothers don't get
none in this movie
produced by Ronald
Bass
I'm Alex Gates in
"Blood & Wine"
a Latina, Gabriella
spends most of her
scenes in bed awaiting
me or my step son
She's balling both of us
She's modest next to
Frankie Donnenfield
(Eva Mendes) in
"The Bad Lieutenant: Port
of Call" she is willing to
satisfy all comers including
her lover detective Terence
McDonagh
But she's chaste in
comparison to Chantel
Eddie Dugan's ho
in "Brooklyn's Finest"
When he shows up for
his appointment she's
with another client
and tells Eddie to wait
Her back is an assembly
line of the skin
But once in awhile
I'd get tired of white,
black, brown, red and
yellow
I want something say

blue
I'm Jake Sully
in Avatar
The Na'vi women
go for me
But I'll have nothing
less than the head man's
daughter
I defeat their proudest
warrior and tame their
most feared monster
And then. Lucky
they
I give them my
DNA
With women throughout
The Milky Way
I have my way

Going For Seventy-Five

for Yuqing Lin

Alex Honnold climbs with no rope nor gear
He breaks between the meadow and stars
His youthful zest plays chicken with fear
He chalks his hands to grip the rock
And reaches El Capitan's top block by block

We've scaled the cliffs and are climbing down
We nod as the Honnolds pass us by
They dazzle the crowd that's
Made the trip
While we dangle by our fingertips
We made some missteps
In our day
Ducked the boulders of our time
Came through the mists and fog
Okay
Survived to climb another day
Our ups and downs are quite a few
But few of them have had our vista
The silverfish have swarmed us too
And we too have sometimes

113

Forgotten our glue
And often we're cut
And other times we bleed
The older we get the less rope we need
Our destination is among the weeds

The Thing Between Us

In the winter
this roomy ghetto
Queen Anne is hard to heat
Made of Oak and Maple it
survived the big one of '06.
You were made of plastic
and survived only two years
Those were good years for us
On that last night
we surfed until 3
I held you in my hand
but the next morning
your place between
me and her was empty
I saw the wrinkles where you usually lay
Instead, you were next to the bed
busted up
all of your parts scattered
your double A batteries
resting at the brink of
the grate
In a panic
I tried to reassemble you

but only made matters worse
Satellite TV sent me an "upgrade"
boy, is it sleek, post modern
a candidate for the Whitney
It's plastic like you
but while you were all black
it is blue with pretty
red green yellow
buttons
It just doesn't have your feel

It was a Sad Day In May

Throughout the City of Angels
In restaurants, barbershops, airport bars and markets
In Sherman Oaks, Brentwood, South Central
Beverly Hills, Culver City and Echo Park
All "seventy two suburbs in search of a city"
Wherever fans gathered, wherever they parked it
Los Angeles wept as the Great Lakers
Were swept

It was a sad day in May when the
Lakers were blown away

They came to the semifinals with a streak of
Seventeen to one
And so many analysts predicted that the Lakers
Should have won
Cause coach Phil Jackson would call
Plays that were wise and were sound
Like a sagacious Zen priest from across
The pond

It was a sad day in May when the
Lakers were blown away

With Kobe, Gasol, Fisher and Artest
They were the team to beat
Second seed in the West
But the wild West is anti-hierarchist
Historians agree
Upstart Memphis grizzled the Spurs
With gusto and glee

With the Lakers down two
Still the fans had hope
Maybe this was the Lakers doing a rope a dope
Maybe a secret plan was in the works
That LA wanted to be the first to beat the curse
That no team could bounce back after losing
Three
This would be the sweetest of all victories

It was a sad day in May when the
Lakers were blown away

But, Terry, Stojaković, and Nowitzki and Barea
Had other ideas
And the Lakers reeled from the quartet's might
Their threes rained down like a meteor shower
This caused Odom and Bynum to get real sour
By the fourth quarter they were ready to rumble
Upset and dazed by the Mavericks' power
Embarrassed by their repeated stumbles
Their inability to get shots to go down

Over popcorn, chips, hotdogs and beer
There was little for Lakers fans to cheer

It was a sad day in May when the

Lakers were blown away
Now Phil has taken his place with the Knicks
And Fisher strolled the sidelines as the Knicks
Took their licks
And Kobe did his long goodbye
And slowly dribbled toward the basketball Hall of
Fame
We their fans can be forever thankful
For the slam dunks and ally oops they brought to
The game
The fast breaks, pick and rolls and buzzer beaters
Galore, but as with all great things
It couldn't last
(Why even Sugar Shane was done the night
Before)
And now L.A. has "blown up" and revised
Buying a new set of legs, hands and arms
Under the guidance of Professor LeBron
And fading from memory as
Rookies are set to play
Is that sad day in May when the
Lakers were blown away

This Girl Is On Fire

The 2013 Grammy's
were too Red State for my
tastes. I'm still back there with
Sarah Vaughn, Ben Webster
and Nat King Cole
I prefer the curmudgeon
as in "Cool Down Papa
Don't You Blow Your Top"

It took Alicia Keys
to wake me up
to set me dreaming
This figure in bronze with hips
by Lachaise
She is wearing the helmet
with two horns
She is mounted on a skittish
black horse
her ankles ringed with
white orchids

drums on each side
she is beating one drum
after another
leading us to war

Nina's lips
are painted on her shield
her heart is on fire
there's smoke in her
eyes

She is right
She is inflammatory
She is combustible
She is an erupting
sun flare
We are cave people
rubbing sticks together
She is the soaring Firebird
bearing down on Chelyabinsk
setting off car alarms
dogs howling
crying babies

She is TNT's sister

next time there's a
blackout in New York
Don't call Con Ed
Call Alicia Keys

What Ails My Apricot Tree

You know the story
He grew up in one of these
FDR housing experiments
There is a photo of him
As a poor boy
Standing in a courtyard
Which is as sterile
as the one at
Pelican Bay

How did Drake put it:
"*Started from the bottom
now we here.*"

Here has brought him a gardener
who prunes his apple, lemon and
gingko trees

They breed like chickens but
The apricot tree hadn't budged
in two years
Was it missing its roots in Armenia?
Still mourning its mother who
who was taken down by termites?

"Is it dead" he asked Mr. Phan
who invited him to stand
before the tree and pointing to the
green on its branches and caressing
its new limbs like one would
caress the face of a horse
It's alive! he said
The next week white flowers
began to appear

Like many of us
all that it needed was some
love

Untitled #5

Buffalo, New York
is like a comatose patient that
revives from time to time to
jog through Humboldt Parkway

Warriors

Life will not always favor you with
Three-pointers, sometimes
You have to take it
To the paint

Not only will the opposing
Team
Commit flagrants
So will those who pose
As impartial

There are times when you
Must speak up even if it
Means drawing a technical
On your job or
In face of an injustice
Or standing up to a bully

You won't always get the free throws
That you think you deserve
In that case
Let the ball do your talking

It's better to be a team player
Than a ball hogger

A deliberate passing of
The ball until the best
Shot is available is
Just as important as
Spectacular fast breaks
And layups in other words
Think before you act

All of us have had our
fourth quarters when
We're down and there
Are a few seconds to go
Be like the Warriors
Never be deflated
Someone in your
Corner might come
Through for you

If you're the best you're
Going to bring out the best
In others
Never underestimate
Your opponent no matter how
Much their losses out
Number their wins

Regardless of heights that
You reach
The records broken
The MVP awards
There will always be critics
Even those without a ring

Don't kick a hole into the
Wall because you lost
There's always the next
Game

Though not as crowd
Pleasing
A solid defense is as important
As a dazzling offense

It's not always about you
It's about the children in
The hospitals whom you
Visit
It's about the high schoolers
Who look up to you
It's about the poor who
Receive turkeys from you
At Christmas
It's about the fans who will
Brave a hurricane to
Cheer you on

Warrrrrriorrrrorssss!!!
Warrrrrriorrriorssss.!!!

Eavesdropping on the Gods

for Elizabeth and Professor Peter André Bloch

Nietzsche lived so far above sea level
that he eavesdropped on the gods
In the bedroom of the white
farm house surrounded by white
mountains captured in Giovanni
Giacometti's "Snow Mountains."
More Olympian
than the gods, he struggled with
Apollo and Dionysus, the Ethiopian
"who came from the south"
The god of mass hysteria
The god of the medulla
Who drove Lycurgus mad
Who drove the daughters of
Minyas mad
Who drove the women of
Argos mad
All because they didn't like to
party

He drove Nietzsche mad.
And, by 1889, he was
signing his letters "Dionysus."
But most of his time he
was Apollonian.

He was a professor
who trimmed his beard
designed a syllabus
wore Gesellschaftsanzug at
faculty dinners and attended
conferences where they talked about
Hegel

He might have wished to be
roaming
the world with a nasty crew.
Maybe like the scene in Selvin's
Altamont. A bunch of winos high
on rotgut.
Wilde Frauen in Nazi boots
dancing to Hard Rock!
Everybody infused with meth
Eating animals without cooking them
and satyrs on Harley Davidson's
who didn't need Viagra.

But when awake
Nietzsche had gastrointestinal
issues
He farted a lot
had failing eyesight
migraines, some would call
him a weakling

a mama's boy
wishing that he
was the Ubermensch
like swaggering Schwarzenegger
after an injection of
Primobolan, Deca Durabolin, and Dianabol.
The grade B Zarathustra
Kurt Wilhelm's friend
"I would invite him to
my wedding," Arnold said of
Wilhelm.

Nietzsche wanted to hang out
with the Mina women
in Dahomey play drums
with the
Halakki Gowda at Karnataka
But no song and dance man, he
No Teutonic Knight, either
He preferred the teacher's ruler
to the bayonet
A chicken hawk
He loved the Greeks but
could sound like
a backwater Manichee
In a long letter to his mom
dated October, 1872, he wrote
"There I dine in my hotel.
Where I already find a
few companions for the
Splugen trip the next day,
they include, unfortunately,
a Jew."

Peter put us up in
the cellar apartment
of Nietzsche-Haus.

I imagined Nietzsche upstairs
dreaming of Siegfried while
sharpening pencils
in Sils Maria
Near Saint Moritz
the former farm town
whose farmers' snow sleds have been
replaced by Rolls Royces
But by the next morning
his Dionysian was exhausted
He was back to preparing a lecture
placing papers in a briefcase
wiping his glasses
and lunching at Frau Dursch's
Corned beef, crisp bread,
Sardines, eggs, tea, and hot water

At Peter's house
Elizabeth fed us Spaghetti Bolognese,
cheeses, panna cotta, fruits, and ice cream.
Nila, his Golden Lab
barked at departed relatives
because the dog knows that after death
we leave our scents behind
He is on spirit patrol in Peter's house
where we talk about the Giacometti

Diego, Alberto, Giovanni, Annetta, Ottilia, Annette
"family"
all of them busy making furniture, jewelry

and art when not posing for each other
Unlike Nietzsche they were
Swiss practical
They could distinguish
between myth, dreams and reality
which is why Alberto was excommunicated
from the surrealists and argued with
Picasso
The waistline of his "Running Man" envied by
Jenny Craig
Giovanni was kept in the shadows
by the fame of Alberto and Diego but
when it came to painting suns, he
brought the light
He brought it!
The sun above Peter's house is the same as
it was when Giovanni painted "Children In The Sun"
or that splash of sun in "Mountain Landscape, I"
so glaring that it could have been painted
with butter
The sun is so bright at Peter's house
that it pulls up a chair
and has a bite

Cold Paul Ryan*

Gil Scott-Heron, you spoke of
Winter in America
But the winter in America is not
As cold as the winter in
Paul Ryan's soul
Paul Ryan is so cold that the
Penguins honored him with an ice statue
Paul Ryan is so cold that when
His colleagues have a meeting with
Him they bring space heaters
Paul Ryan is so cold that when
He breathes on somebody they
Get frostbitten
Paul Ryan is so cold that his
Nickname in high school was
32 Degrees F
Or simply 32
Paul Ryan is so cold that
Jack Frost sued him for
Identity theft

Paul Ryan told a dying man
No more medicine for you
We need that bed for a VIP
Your bill is way overdue
Insurance companies
Pay my way?
What is that to you?
All of my colleagues
Are up for sale
Owned by the guys
Who are too big to jail
When I go out to dine
On crab
The Kochs, and Big Pharma
Pick up the Tab

Paul Ryan drinks a
Wine called
Echezeaux Grand Cru
350 a bottle to order
To you
A long way from
Janesville, WI., population
62,640
When he cuts the safety net
You'll fall in love with pigeon stew
You'll be scouring through
Garbage cans for food of any
Description
You'll become shoplifters
In drugstores to fill your prescriptions
All of you marks who voted for Trump
You'll be sub primed and thrown out
On your fat spoiled hateful rumps

I'm taking away your
Social Security he told
The seniors who
Get their news from
Fox
You'd better hold
On to your puny savings
To pay for that final box
God forbid your kids get
Sick from the chicken pox
You'd better have some money
To spare
Because Paul Ryan got rid
Of Obamacare

Paul Ryan is so cold that the
Penguins dedicated an ice statue to him

He's going to privatize your
Medicare
He's going to
Privatize
Your cat
If you don't watch out
He might even privatize your
Mama now what do you
Think about that
Now, do you miss Barack Obama?

Paul Ryan is a cold cold dude
He has an icebox for a
Heart
He does his abs in the Capitol gym
To trim away his flab

But he hogs all he can from
Big oil and gas
The 1% own his skinny ass
He's so inhuman that he's
Never used the loo
He doesn't have ice in his veins
He's lacking in veins
And in blood cells too
Ice Tea won't get anywhere near
Paul Ryan
Nor will Ice Cube
And when the Republican Party
Melts down all of the ice the
Only glaciers remaining
Will be found in Paul Ryan's
Eyes

But this altar boy will face his
God one day
And She'll say you got the wrong
Address Representative Paul Ryan
You need to go the other way

Paul Ryan is so cold that the
Penguins dedicated an ice statue to him
Paul Ryan is so cold that when
His colleagues have a meeting with
Him they bring space heaters
Paul Ryan's idea of a vacation
Is Buffalo in December
Paul Ryan is so cold that when
He breathes on somebody they
Get frost
Bitten. Have to have

Their fingers amputated
Paul is so cold that his
Nickname in high school was
32 Degrees F
Or just 32
Paul Ryan is so cold that
Jack Frost sued him for
Identity theft

*Former Speaker of the House of Representatives and
fan of Ayn Rand

Pluto and Luca Walk into a Bar

Pluto overhears Luca say
Why aren't I given credit for
All life that exists?
Is it because
I'm a single-cell, bacterium-like organism?
I, who am the ancestor of trees, birds, fish
And just about everything that you
Can think of
Instead of looking to the sky for
God, they should look to the bottom
Of the ocean where I live

O, you think that you don't get
Respect, Pluto said
First, they gave me that
Dreadful name after the
Greek Hades and then
They dismiss me as
Just a big snowball in space

And now that they find I'm more
Complicated
That underneath my surface
Lie oceans and possibly life
I'm booted from the news cycle
by the discovery of a 9th planet

Turning to the bartender
A pigeon, Pluto said
At least we're not a pigeon

The pigeon
Was unruffled, he said
Calmly, wiping some glasses
"Well, Pluto, it must be
Scary to be on a
Collision course with Neptune
Whom do you think will prevail
From such an encounter?

And Luca, you have to have
One of Jacques Cousteau, Jr's
Submersibles to even
Notice you
Down there cold, dark and
Lonely

You will never see a rainbow
While my neck is one

Red Summer, 2015

The year is 2015
Nine Christians are shot
by a man with a scheme
He was nurtured and
weaned on
a textbook of lies
which honored slavers
Jefferson Davis
Nathan Bedford Forrest
And Robert E. Lee

The devil entered
Vesey's church
Disguised as a youth
The Christians took notice
Of his hoof for a foot
But everybody was welcome
even Daniel Roof
His mind full of bile

He martyred his hosts
a mother played dead
in the blood of her child
But the holy ones prayers with
their African roots
Almost moved
Young Roof
"almost had me shouting on my
feet that I almost forgot
my heinous deed."

A child was shot down
while holding a toy
The police asked questions
but nobody was blamed
The stars in his eyes went
dim in the day
He lay on the pavement
where children play

A man was shot
while running away
The shooter took aim
as though he were game

The demons are partying
with their buddies, the
fiends and having a good
time
Red Summer
the year is
2015

For making ends meet
by selling cigs loose
or making a lane change
they will give you the noose

Before his final heave
Eric Garner said
I can't breathe
his neck was crushed
he could breathe no more
they found Sandra dead on
the jailhouse floor
a grand jury looked
and issued a tome
they blessed the killers
and allowed them to roam

When Dorsey got news
that both wife and child were
dead
that's our mood
in this summer of dread
The spirit was his guide
when he wrote that great song
but who is the god
who will take our hand
and who is the god
who will lead us on
"Don't you get weary"
Martin said when he
spoke of his dream
his words have kept us
from drowning in screams
in this bloody summer

of 2015
where killers and murderers
reign supreme

You brought down the flag
You all joined hands and
cried
but you still have
highways and buildings
honoring those who
committed high crimes
who didn't want people to
be free
Jefferson Davis
Nathan Bedford Forrest
and
Robert E. Lee

The Gingko Tree

I don't need a dog
I have a Gingko tree
The advantage is that
I don't have to take it for
A walk.

Dialog

JEdgar: Martin, I understand that you like to party?
When is the next one?
MLK: You want the address?
JEdgar: I already have the address.

Blu

(A Yuricane Poem)

Your ponytail and artsy jeans don't
Fool me
I remember when you bought your
First pair of shoes
You were nineteen
These women don't belong to you anymore
You can't use them as an excuse
To burn up people like you
Use to
They can be with whom they wish to
Be with
Nowadays, your nooses are only symbolic
You're at the end of your rope

We use to call your type RedNecks
And Crackers until we found that they
Were terms meant to hurt poor white people
Like the turnip growers in Caldwell's *Tobacco Road*,
And the mine workers in Conroy's *The Disinherited*
The single mother in Tillie Olson's "I Stand Here
Ironing"

William Kennedy's strikers
In those days disenfranchised meant more
Than an excuse to pardon the parish that
Voted for David Duke

But there are different sides of Georgia

There's Ray Charles's "Georgia"
There's Atlanta's "Mall of America"
There's Morehouse and Spellman

And then there's your Georgia
The Georgia where your grandpappy
A snaggle-toothed hater stands
In his mud spattered brogans
Grinning below the dangling twitching
Feet of a Black man
In "100 Years of Lynching"
The only difference between him
And you is that
He never heard of John Cage

In his Georgia
Squirrel meat was
A delicacy
And you could make a cap out of
Raccoon fur
And you were judged by how far
You could spit

But now you have moved uptown from
Your Georgia roots
Or shall we say downtown where you
Have a position among the avant garde

Lighting up the stage
You've moved from Dr. Pepper to
White wine

Man, are you cutting edge
You the new thing
But as your Yankee wife
Prepares a candlelight dinner
Accompanied by a string quartet
Don't you wish it was that old
Flea scratching hounddog
Baying in the hills

Just Rollin' Along

L.C. "Good Rockin'" Robinson (born Louis Charles Robinson; May 13, 1914-September 26, 1976) was an American blues singer, guitarist, and fiddle player. "He played an electric steel guitar. Robinson was more than just a storyteller. He was one of the Bay Area's most significant blues artists,....who helped shape what's come to be known as West Coast Blues. When Robinson died in 1976, [Ron] Steward recounts, the influential bluesman was near penniless and friends had to pass a hat around at his funeral."
Jim Harrington

It was '34 Oklahoma and L.C. was doing a gig
People were doing the Texas Two Step
And greasing on the pig
There were mounds upon mounds of ice cream
The pies were crusty and fine
The following story is true and I ain't lyin'
Good Rockin' Robinson was packing them in
But the noise of a Ford sedan disrupted the
Din
A woman and a man
The man had a grin

They were
Just rollin' along
Just rollin' along

Her lap held a Thompson
The barrel was long
"I'll give you 12 silver dollars," she said
"If you play our song"
"I'm sitting on top of the world"
"I'm sitting on top of the world"

They were
Just rollin' along
Just rollin' along

They paid Good Rockin' and
Were on their way
Very few in the crowd will forget that
Day
The policeman pulled up
He was all out of breath
"Did you see a couple in a Ford
Come this way?
She was dapper," he said
"He wore a Newsboy cap
And a pistol on his side"

Good Rockin' asked who was
In that ride
The policeman said
"It was Bonnie and Clyde"
The policeman said
"It was Bonnie and Clyde"
They were
Just rollin' along
Just rollin' along

Ethel at 100

For Ethel Strasser, (1917-2018)

The Quaker state offered your family refuge
From the hairy grasp of a mean Czar
Pittsburgh was a steel town, and you had
To be as firm as that metal as you girded
Against a Depression and World Wars
Like Thelma, my mom
You tolerated the foolish men
A ceiling that was not glass but
Brick
Like hers
Your career goals were stunted
Yet

You raised four girls, virtually alone
Which meant that while middle class
Families consulted travel agents
You were burning the midnight oil
Consulting coupons
Stretching the dollar
Making do
Cutting corners and then there

Was the chicken pox
Mononucleosis
Measles
And symptoms that are yet
To be diagnosed and then
The dance lessons
The violin lessons
Art Lessons
Plus the boyfriends

Ethel Strasser
Your job at Carnegie Tech qualified
The children for free education
Like Thelma, you were a 1917er
Born in a world even
Messier than now
Something about which the
Millenns
Have no notion as they sip
Their Blonde Cappuccinos
Peer over their tablets
And chat on Facebook
About their cats
And now you are 100
A survivor from a period
During which millions of
Your sisters perished

They are having
A party for you at
Blauvelt, New York's
Oscar's Italian Restaurant

Your daughters are there
Women of high distinction
Gail, Sonya, Carla and Judith
"The pride of Pittsburgh"

Their children are there
And grandchildren
And great-grandchildren
Who could form
A subcommittee for the U.N.,
The youngest, Lina, corrects her teacher's
Japanese

We have a choice of fish or
Veal
There are drinks
All around
And when they wheeled
You in
Below the hush that
Filled the room
I thought I heard
An angel whisper
That Ethel !
That Ethel !

Blues Christmas

For Chole and Doshi

She hurt me so bad on Christmas Eve
I cried all Christmas Day
She hurt me so bad on Christmas Eve
That I cried all Christmas Day
She told me that she'd had enough
I pleaded for her to stay

I'm tired of your lies, your drinking and
Your fooling around, she said
Your downtown yellow whore
I tried to tell her to give me some time
She said, you've promised all that before

She hurt me so bad on Christmas Eve
That I cried all Christmas Day
She hurt me so bad on Christmas Eve
That I cried all Christmas Day
When I got home at 2 a.m.
She told me that she'd had enough
I tried my best to get her to stay

My Christmas is worse than merry
George Dickel can't cheer me up
There's black snow on the driveway
And Santa won't get no soup
No presents under the Christmas tree
No jingle bells and elves
My head feels like a volcano
My head's beginning to swell

When you get a good woman
You take for granted
There's so much that they will take
They know the difference between
An upright man and a low down
Dirty skank
So next time you're seeking pleasure
And leaving it all over the earth
Your Christmas dinner will be day old pizza
And you won't get no dessert

Ishmael Reed   Copyright©2018

Carla at 77

That Neutrinos
Are the quirkiest of
All particles is a
Theory about which
Few physicists quarrel

Quicker than Mercury
I could have been a
Neutrino

Born in the Sun

But I would be a
A queer particle
Going it alone
I'd hardly matter

You and I are Quarks
Quarks come in pairs
Like Scarlet Macaws

The Milky Way is a Hot Head

The Milky Way is named for spilled
Breast milk, but is no milk-toast
Like a school yard bully who
left a smaller kid seeing stars
The Milky Way crashed into
A dwarf galaxy
Ten billion years ago
Which is why the Milky Way
Has an expanded waistline
Astronomers
Call the victim
"The Gaia Sausage"
The Milky Way thinks like you
and me
Shooting stars
Like a child shoots marbles
It knew what it was doing

When he's away from home he cheats
Instead of his daily oatmeal
Sausage lies on a tray
Next to plates of whole wheat
toast, jam, and a pot of coffee

He can't imagine what
A sausage-like galaxy looks like
A sausage dwarf
Was it shaped like a quarter moon?
Or round like a full moon
Did it look like the sausage
They serve in Chattanooga along
With a side of grits?
Would it resemble the sausage
laying on his plate derived not
from hogs, but from a turkey?
A Yankee version of sausage?
But when the Milky Way
Nightly invites our eyes to dine
On her wonders
Who cares about how
The sausage is made
So why does the Milky Way
have nightmares?
Because it will never erase
the traces of its crime

The Ultimate Security

What would happen if I had
A couple of dragons to back me up
Like Sophie Turner in "Game of Thrones"
I only need one
When I'm standing
In a line that stretches into last week
My dragons show up and I'm
Next

When I'm having a loud argument with
Relatives who've overstayed their visit
My dragon's head would enter the front
Door and they'd pack their bags

You know the fella across
The street who parks his
Middle-aged crisis red Corvette
In front of my house when
There's plenty of room in
Front of his?
He would be running screaming
And shaking his fist at the sky

As my dragon was delivering his
Car to the junkyard

The 3 pit bulls that menace
My neighborhood
No problem
Car break-ins
No problem
The guy whose car's
Bass rattles the street
Covered

The money that I'd spend
On alarms
Can be spent at
GrubHub.

How would I solve
The Oakland drug
Crisis
My dragons would shut down
The Port of Oakland

How would I feed my dragon
I'd give him the names
And addresses
Of all of my critics

The Black Hole Sings The Blues

"In musical terms, the pitch of the sound generated by the black hole translates into the note of B flat." NASA Science

Black Hole
I can understand why your
Song is in B flat
The root note of your
Typical piano blues
Here you are munching away at
Anything that comes near you
Like an extraterrestrial shark
Your favorite dish is light
Left alone you had the worlds
on your plate
Just a
Theory in the professor's head
You had it good
That didn't last
Here they come the paparazzi
With giant lenses
Only they call themselves
EHT team

They've made you a star
But even though you
Can swallow a pile of suns

It's all about them
These ants under the
Front porch
The "little me" in the
Song by Mary Wells

"What would happen
If we fall in?" they want to
Know
Earthworms, the Black
Hole holed up Messier 87
53 million light years from
Earth
Ain't studying you
They gave you a flat dull
technical name
They should call you
BESSIE

The End

Acknowledgements: Published and Unpublished

Moving Richmond
        Commissioned by the City of Richmond. The poem
        is broken up and is installed in two huge blocks
        of faceted steel sculptures by Mildred Howard,
        mounted on the walls of Richmond's Bay Area Rapid
        Transit Station (BART), in Richmond, where they
        greet commuters each day.

Gustav
        Unpublished

If I Am A Welfare Queen
        Recorded as spoken word by Ishmael Reed, on the
        CD *For All We Know* (Ishmael Reed Publishing Co.,
        2007) by The Ishmael Reed Quintet, featuring David
        Murray as composer/performer

Untitled #1
        Unpublished

Untitled #2
        Unpublished

Hope Is A Thing With Feathers
        Recorded on *Be My Monster Love* (Motéma, 2012) by
        David Murray and the Infinity Quartet, with vocal
        by Gregory Porter

Hip Hop and The Blues
Unpublished

The Diabetic Dreams Of Cake
The Paris Review, #218, Fall 2016   (63-66)

My Colon and Metamucil Get Married
Unpublished

Why I Will Never Write A Sonnet
Cody, Judith, Kim McMillon and Claire Ortalda, editors: *Fightin' Words: 25 Years of Provocative Poetry and Prose from "The Blue Collar Pen"* (Oakland: 2014) (125)

Sweet Pea

2011 -l'Art du Jazz. Paris, France: Editions du Fein, 2016; and in *Of Poetry & Protest: from Emmett Till to Trayvon Martin*, edited and compiled by Philip Cushway and MichaelWarr (WW Norton, 2016) (154-157)

Love is a natural feeling
Performed by Macy Gray Sep 10, 2011 - During Jazz à la Villette festival, Red Bull Music Academy; and recorded on *Be My Monster Love* (Motéma, 2012) by David Murray and the Infinity Quartet, with vocal by Macy Gray

Prayer of a Nigerian Official
Vocal performed by Tony Allen September 10, 2011 - During Jazz à la Villette festival, Red Bull Music Academy

Army Nurse
Recorded as spoken text by Ishmael Reed, set to music by David Murray on the CD, *For All We Know* (Ishmael Reed Publishing Co, 2007), with The Ishmael Reed Quintet

Honoring My Closest Friends
Unpublished

Those pesky things called genes
>   *Unpublished*

Untitled #3
>   *Unpublished*

If I Were A Hospice Worker
>   Recorded as "Africa" on *The Devil Tried to Kill Me*
>   (Justin Time Records, 2007), set to music by David
>   Murray with vocal by Taj Mahal

House on Belgrave Street
>   *Unpublished*

The Jazz Martyrs
>   Appeared in an earlier version, as "Who Are the Jazz
>   Martyrs," in *Black Renaissance Noire*, Volume 14,
>   Issue 1 Spring/Summer 2014 (42-49)

Red Summer, 2015
>   Recorded on *blues for memo* (Doublemoon Records,
>   2016) set to music as "Red Summer" by David
>   Murray and sung by Pervis Evans;
>   and appears in Rimondi, Giorgio, editor: *il grande
>   incantatore per Ishmael Reed* (Milano: Agenzia X,
>   2016), a commemorative documentation of the
>   2016 Alberto Dubito International Prize awarded to
>   Reed in Venice, where it is also translated into Italian
>   by Sergio Garau as "Estate Rossa, 2015" (146-155)

The Banishment
>   *Unpublished*

The Return
>   *Unpublished*

Hit and Run
>   Shuck, Kim and Karla Brundage, editors. *Oakland
>   Out Loud, Poetry and Prose in Celebration of 'There.'*
>   Oakland: Jukebox Press, 2007, (7-8)

Capitalism Throws Me A Banquet
>Published in Rimondi, Giorgio, editor: *Il grande incantatore per Ishmael Reed* (Milano: Agenzia X, 2016) with an Italian translation by Marco Fazzini as 'Il capitalismo mi offre un lauto pranzo" (156-159)

The Oakland Developer
>*Unpublished*

Eulogy for Carl Tillman
>*Unpublished*

Untitled #4
>*Unpublished*

The Missionaries
>Recorded as "Army of the Faithful (Joyful Noise)" on *Be My Monster Love* (Motéma, 2012) by David Murray and the Infinity Quartet with vocal by Gregory Porter

Mino Woman
>Recorded on *New Throned King* (5Passion, 2014), by composer and musician Yosvany Terry and nominated for 2015 Grammy, Best Latin Jazz album

Scrub Jays
>*Slate* magazine, August 9, 2011, selected by Robert Pinsky

Myron
>*Unpublished*

Be My Monster, love
>Recorded on the CD *Be My Monster Love* (Motéma, 2012) by David Murray and the Infinity Quartet with vocal by Macy Gray

Choices
>*Unpublished*

If I Were A White Leading Man
>*Black Renaissance Noire*, Volume 11, Issue 1, Spring 2011 (58-59)

Going For Seventy Five
> *Word, an anthology by A Gathering of the Tribes*. A Gathering of the Tribes, 2017 (63)

The Thing Between Us
> *Unpublished*

It was a Sad Day In May
> *Unpublished*

This Girl Is On Fire
> *Unpublished*

What Ails My Apricot Tree
> *Unpublished*

Untitled #5
> *Unpublished*

Warriors
> *The San Francisco Chronicle*, February 14, 2016

Eavesdropping on The Gods
> In Ludwig, Sämi, editor: *American Multiculturalism in Context: Views from at Home and Abroad* (Newcastle Upon Tyne, U.K.: Cambridge Scholars Publishing, 2017) (225-229)

Cold Paul Ryan
> Published as "Wisconsin's Paul Ryan" in *Black Renaissance Noire*, Volume 17, Issue 2, Fall, 2017(128-129)

Luca and Pluto Walk Into A Bar
> Published in *Alta: Journal of Alta California*, Spring/2019

The Gingko Tree
> *Unpublished*

Dialog
> *Unpublished*

Music to your Ears
> *Unpublished*

Just Rollin' Along

> Published in *Black Renaissance Noire*, Volume 18 Issue 3, Fall 2018. And chosen by Jackson, Major, guest editor and series editor, David Lehman for *The Best American Poetry 2019*. (New York: Simon & Schuster, 2019)

Ethel at 100

> Published in *Haaretz*, May 30, 2018, accompanied by a video of Reed reading the poem, posted on YouTube May 30, 2018

Blues Christmas

> *Unpublished*

The Milky Way Is A Hot Head

> *Unpublished*

The Ultimate Security

> *Unpublished*

The Black Hole Sings The Blues

> *Unpublished*